IMAGES
of America

BREWING IN
JACKSONVILLE

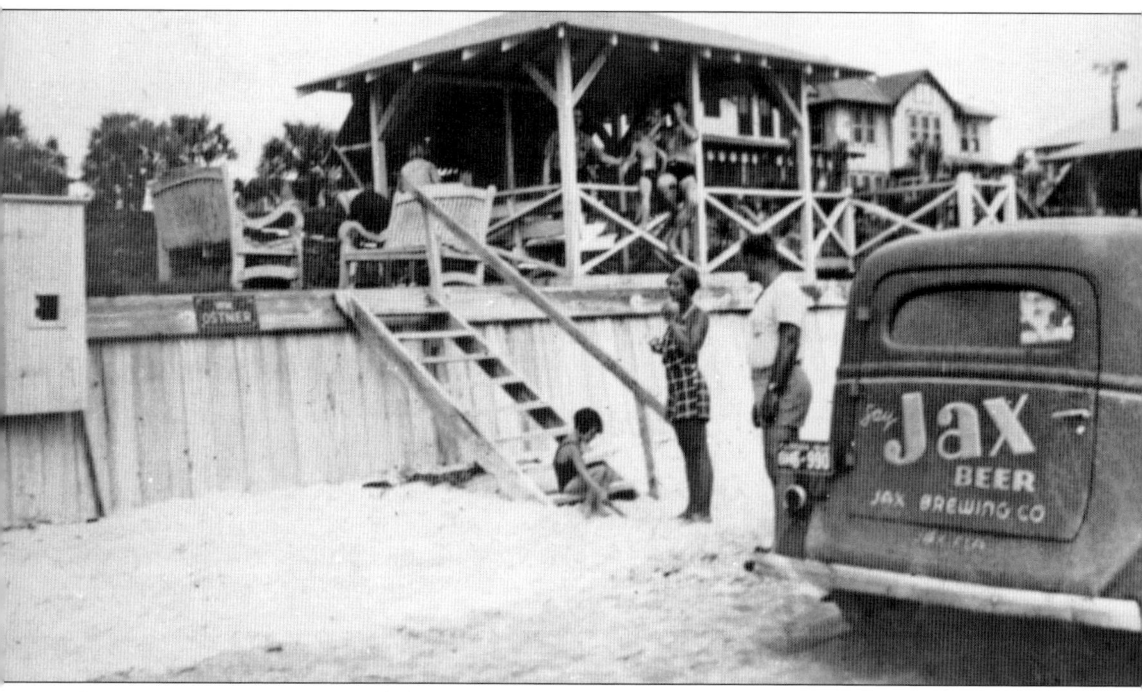

Jax Brewing Company was founded in 1913 by William Ostner, becoming the second brewery to open in Florida. The brewery was known for its Jax Beer German-style pilsner. The photograph shows William Ostner and his family at Jacksonville Beach in the 1930s with a Jax Brewing Company vehicle. (Courtesy of Beaches Museum.)

IMAGES
of America

BREWING IN JACKSONVILLE

Andrew R. Nicholas

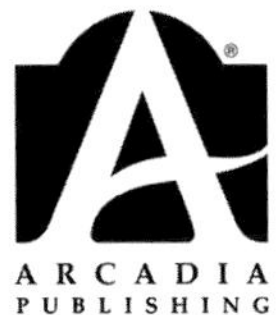

ARCADIA
PUBLISHING

To my cat, Miss Kitty

Contents

Acknowledgments

This book would not have been possible without the following organizations: Jacksonville Historical Society, Jacksonville Public Library, Jacksonville Historical Preservation Commission, Beaches Museum, State Archives of Florida, University of North Florida, Library Company of Philadelphia, Digital Public Library of America, Missouri Historical Society, McNeese State University, Digital Commonwealth Massachusetts Collection Online, and Library of Congress.

I want to especially thank the following people for making all this possible: Sean Bielman; Dennis Espinosa; Bill Delaney; the website the Jaxson; Jessica Jones and the Pink Boots Society; Jim Linn and his website I Stop for Hops; Verance Photography; Beth Learn; Bob Self and his assistance with Loyd Sangren's photography, which is featured on the website Vintage Jacksonville; Stefanie Keeler; Wayne Wood; Sandy Manwell; Leon Winer; Edward Pulido; and Lisa Moody.

The book *Reclaiming Jacksonville: Stories behind the River City's Historic Landmarks*, by Ennis Davis and Robert Mann, provided a wealth of information on William Ostner and Jax Brewing Company and was used as a reference for this publication. Much credit on the history of the building, the brewery, and William Ostner in this publication goes to their own work and research, which can further be found in their beautifully well-made book. Ennis Davis has also done great work in research and writing about Jacksonville history, which has been used as a reference in parts of this publication including on Eggenweiler and Joseph Zapf. *Jacksonville's Architectural Heritage*, by Wayne Wood, was also used as a reference. Tim Gilmore's website Jaxpsychogeo.com with its plethora of information brings great insights into Jacksonville history including some of its breweries.

Thank you to all the modern breweries of Jacksonville and the beaches. I could not fit every photograph of the breweries in this publication, but I do want to mention everyone included and not included here: Ragtime Tavern, River City Brewing Company, Seven Bridges Grille and Brewery, Bold City Brewery, Intuition Ale Works, Engine 15 Brewing Company, Pinglehead Brewing Company, Veterans United Craft Brewery, Wicked Barley Brewing Company, Ruby Beach Brewing Company, Green Room Brewing Company, Congaree & Penn, Hyperion Brewing Company, Atlantic Beach Brewing Company, Fishweir Brewing Company, Southern Swells Brewing Company, Main & Six Brewing Company, Bottlenose Brewing, Tabula Rasa Brewing Company, Reve Brewing Company, Tepeyolot Cerveceria, Lemonstreet Brewing Company, Strings Sports Brewery, Legacy Ale Works, King Maker Brewing, Ink Factory Brewing, Historically Hoppy Brewing Company, Myrtle Avenue Brewing Company, Flying Fish Taphouse, Grace Note Brewing Company, Jekyll Brewing Jax Beach, Voodoo Brewing Company, and Mayport Brewing Company.

Thank you to the bottle shops for providing Jacksonville with access to all our local breweries in convenient locations: Beer:30, Jax Craft Beer, Really Good Beer Stop, Grape & Grain Exchange, 9-Zero-Pour, and Alewife Craft Beer Bottleshop.

Thank you to the Jax Ale Trail brewery passport for showing all the modern breweries of Jacksonville.

INTRODUCTION

Jacksonville was founded in 1822 out of the former settlement on the St. Johns River called Cowford. It is a relatively young city compared to the other major cities where brewing is a dominant feature such as St. Louis and Milwaukee. Jacksonville took its time to become a brewing city, with its first brewer, Eggenweiler & Co. Brewery opening in 1871. And Jacksonville was certainly no Milwaukee. It was Jacksonville—a city that had its saloons and bars lining the dusty road of late-19th-century Bay Street, which revealed that Jacksonville had a love of beer. That love of beer birthed a brewery long gone but not forgotten called the Jax Brewing Company, bearing the nickname of what some locals call Jacksonville, Jax. That love of beer led to the powerhouse Anheuser-Busch establishing its seventh brewery in Jacksonville in 1969. And of course, that love of beer also evolved today into a prodigious lot of microbreweries and craft breweries unforeseen in the history of Jacksonville. The craft breweries raised Jacksonville from the dead of brewing where its past revealed what the city strived to become, a beer capital of Florida. Brewing in Jacksonville shows the history of what the city once was and currently is, including the Jacksonville beaches, from its early days of brewing to modern-day craft breweries.

The brewing industry of Jacksonville began to emerge when larger well-known out-of-state breweries began distributing their products through local business proprietors. Pabst Blue Ribbon, Anheuser-Busch, Old Milwaukee, and Schlitz are some of the more popular breweries to first begin making an impact on the local Jacksonville brewing industry. Although these were not brewed specifically in Jacksonville, they were nonetheless a stepping stone in making the city part of the larger brewing industry. The Jax Brewing Company, opening in 1913 with several years out of commission during Prohibition, put Jacksonville on the brewing map as it became a recognizable brewery in Florida and the southeastern United States. The increased popularity of out-of-state breweries like Anheuser-Busch decreased demand for the local Jax Brewing Company, leading to its closure by 1960.

Anheuser-Busch became the largest brewery in Jacksonville when it established a large plant on the Northside in 1969. The Jacksonville Anheuser-Busch plant has now become the third largest Anheuser-Busch plant in the United States, producing over 9 million barrels of beer per year. A nearby sod farm on Lem Turner Road called Nutri-Turf Land Application Farm is owned by Anheuser-Busch to return wastewater from its Jacksonville brewery to the environment by fertilizing hay and turf crops. Sod purchased from Anheuser-Busch's Nutri-Turf farm is used mostly by golf courses and athletic fields in the southeastern United States. In 2006, Jimmy Buffett established the Margaritaville Brewing Company, known for producing Landshark Lager for his restaurant chain Margaritaville. Buffett's brewery existed in name only, with Landshark Lager being brewed at the Jacksonville Anheuser-Busch plant. The years-long mutual relationship between Anheuser-Busch and the city of Jacksonville still continues to have a positive impact to this day. The Jacksonville Jaguars also have a mutual relationship with Anheuser-Busch, which has become a prominent sponsor of the NFL team.

Attempting to turn itself into a craft beer mecca in the southeastern United States, the history of how Jacksonville got here is rich with intrigue. Modern breweries have several terms to describe their output of production of beer per year. A craft brewery produces no more than 6 million barrels of beer per year. A microbrewery is smaller than a craft brewery, producing less beer at around 15,000 barrels of beer per year. And finally, a nanobrewery produces less than 15,000 barrels of beer per year. The term "modern brewery" in this publication implies that the brewery is either a craft brewery, microbrewery, or nanobrewery unless specifically said otherwise.

The modern breweries of Jacksonville began to appear in the late 20th century when River City Brewing Company emerged on the Southbank of the St. Johns River. Brewing in Jacksonville later exploded in the late 2000s and throughout the 2010s when the early modern breweries, mostly consisting of craft breweries, emerged. To see the impact of the Jacksonville modern brewery industry, simply go to any grocery store in or around North Florida to see these locally brewed products ready for purchase. And, of course, there are events celebrating the breweries and beer culture of Jacksonville, like the Beaches Oktoberfest, Riverside Craft Beer Festival, and the San Marco Beer Festival. As of 2024, there are over 20 breweries in Jacksonville and still going. Unfortunately, several breweries had to close into the 2020s due to factors including the economic effects of the COVID-19 pandemic. Whether in business or closed, each modern brewery contributed to the overall culture of Jacksonville's craft brewery scene, elevating it further to the status as a true beer city.

One

JACKSONVILLE'S OPEN TAB

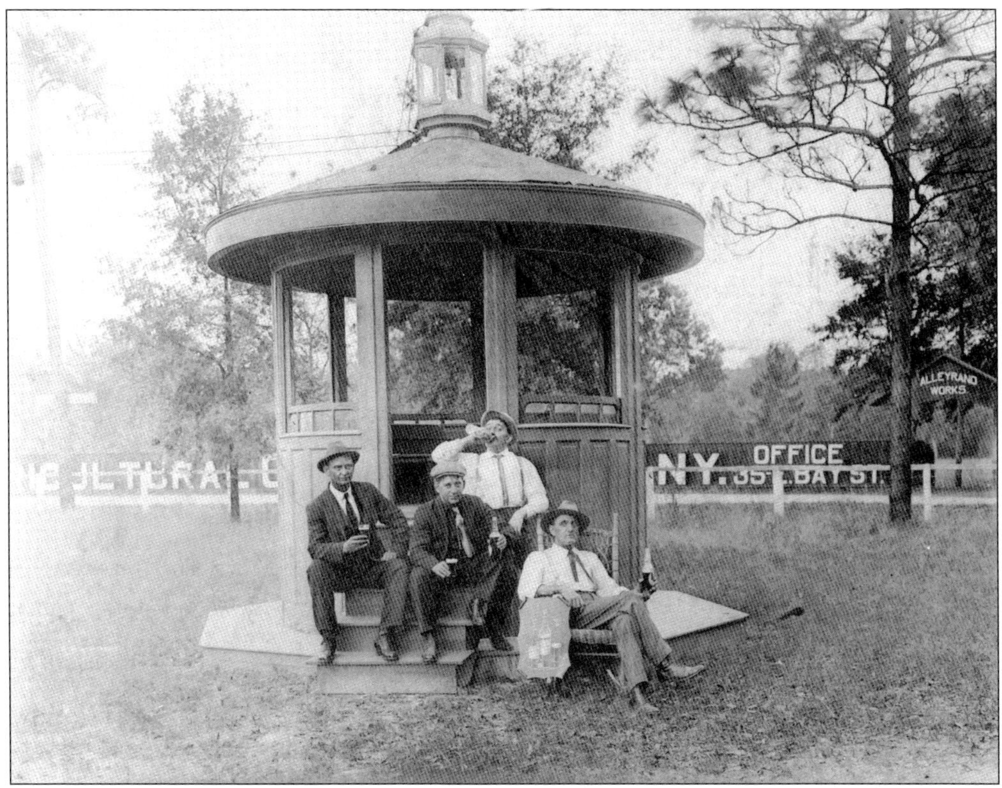

Four men sit in a park drinking beer in the early 1900s. The fence in the back has an unknown advertisement for a business on Bay Street. To the right of that fence is a structure with the words "Talleyrand Works." Talleyrand is an industrial area on the St. Johns River immediately north of the western end of the Mathews Bridge. (Courtesy of Jacksonville Historical Society.)

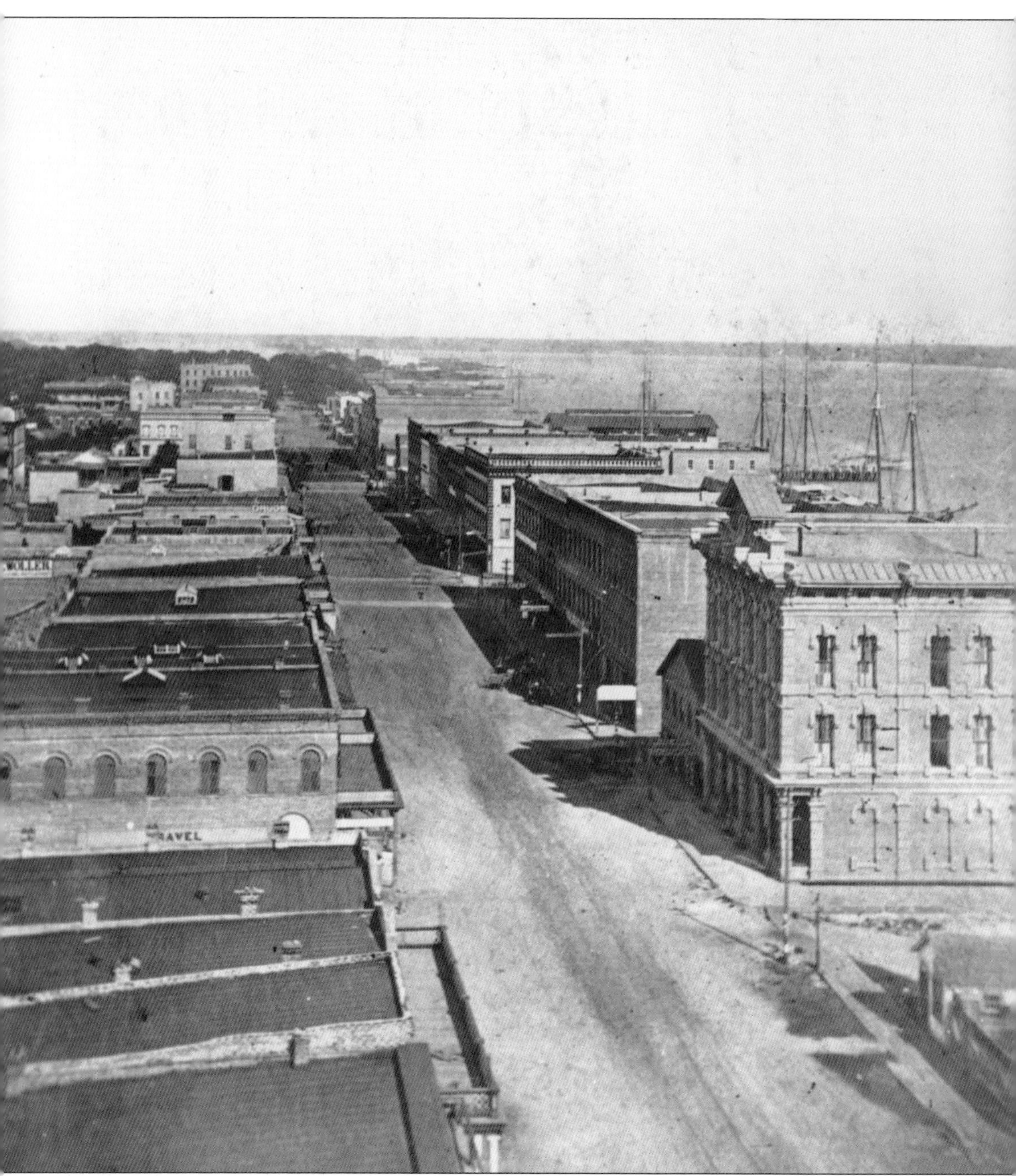

In the 19th century, Bay Street was one of the main roads of Jacksonville, which at the time only encompassed the present-day area of downtown on the north side of the St. Johns River. The photograph shows Bay Street looking east in the 1870s with a view of the St. Johns River flowing east and rounding the bend at Commodore Point. Most bars and saloons in 19th-century Jacksonville were located on Bay Street. Most of the buildings in the photograph were destroyed in the Great Fire of 1901. Today, Bay Street still has its fair share of bars, including one that was featured on the television show *Bar Rescue*. Bold City Breweries' second location opened in 2017 on Bay Street next to the bar and music venue called the Albatross. (Courtesy of State Archives of Florida.)

A beer is an alcoholic beverage made from grain that is fermented with yeast and flavored with hops. In the late 19th century, Jacksonville had the choice of beer between an ale or a lager in local saloons. This advertisement shows a saloon called Fuller's Oyster and Dining Saloon featuring ales, wines, liquors, and segars from 1870. "Segar" is an obsolete spelling of "cigar." (Courtesy of Jacksonville Public Library.)

Brewing in the early 19th century was localized and mostly consisted of ales. Saloons like Lyman's on Bay Street sold ales in the late 1800s. Lyman's saloon was located at the corner of Bay and Pine Streets. An advertisement from Lyman's says it had "choice ales, wines, liquors and segars." This photograph from the 1870s shows a group of people in front of A.B. Hussley groceries with Lyman's in the background. (Courtesy of New York Public Library.)

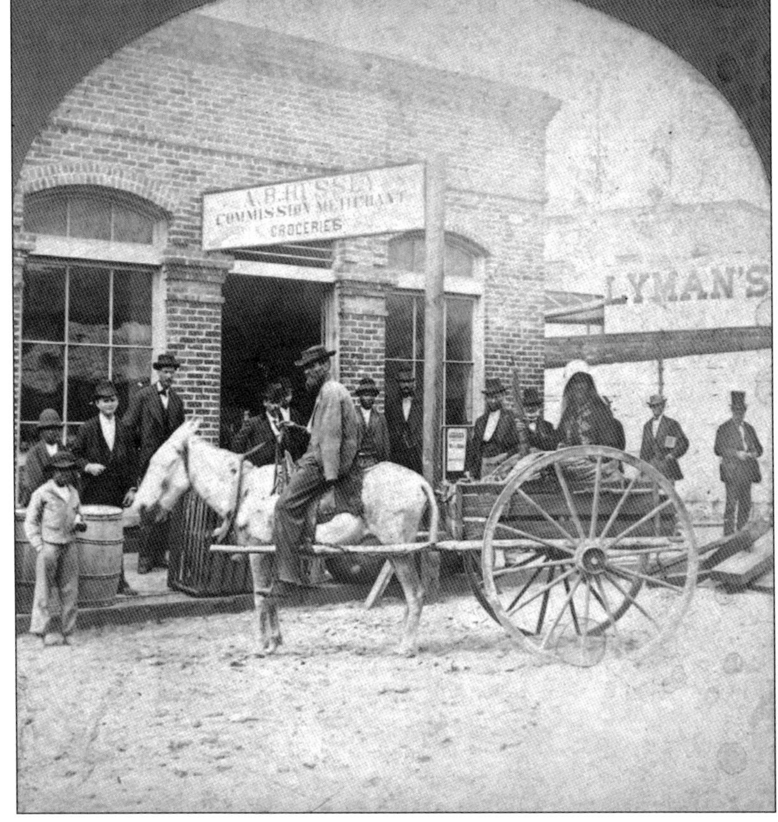

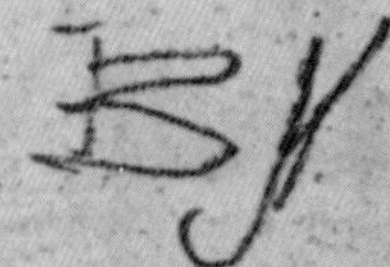

An ale is fermented with top-forming yeast, which turns into a beer at a higher temperature in comparison to lager yeast, which needs colder temperatures. Ales were easier to brew than lagers because they needed warmer temperatures to ferment. An advertisement from 1870 for Philadelphia Ale Depot on Bay Street features ales, wines, and liquors. (Courtesy of Jacksonville Public Library.)

A lager is fermented with bottom-fermenting yeast at cold temperatures. Because lagers are made in cold temperatures, they take longer to ferment—up to eight weeks as compared to ales, which can take about five weeks. The advertisement for the Grand Central Lager Beer Saloon on East Bay Street around 1878 features ales, wines, liquors, and lagers. (Courtesy of Jacksonville Public Library.)

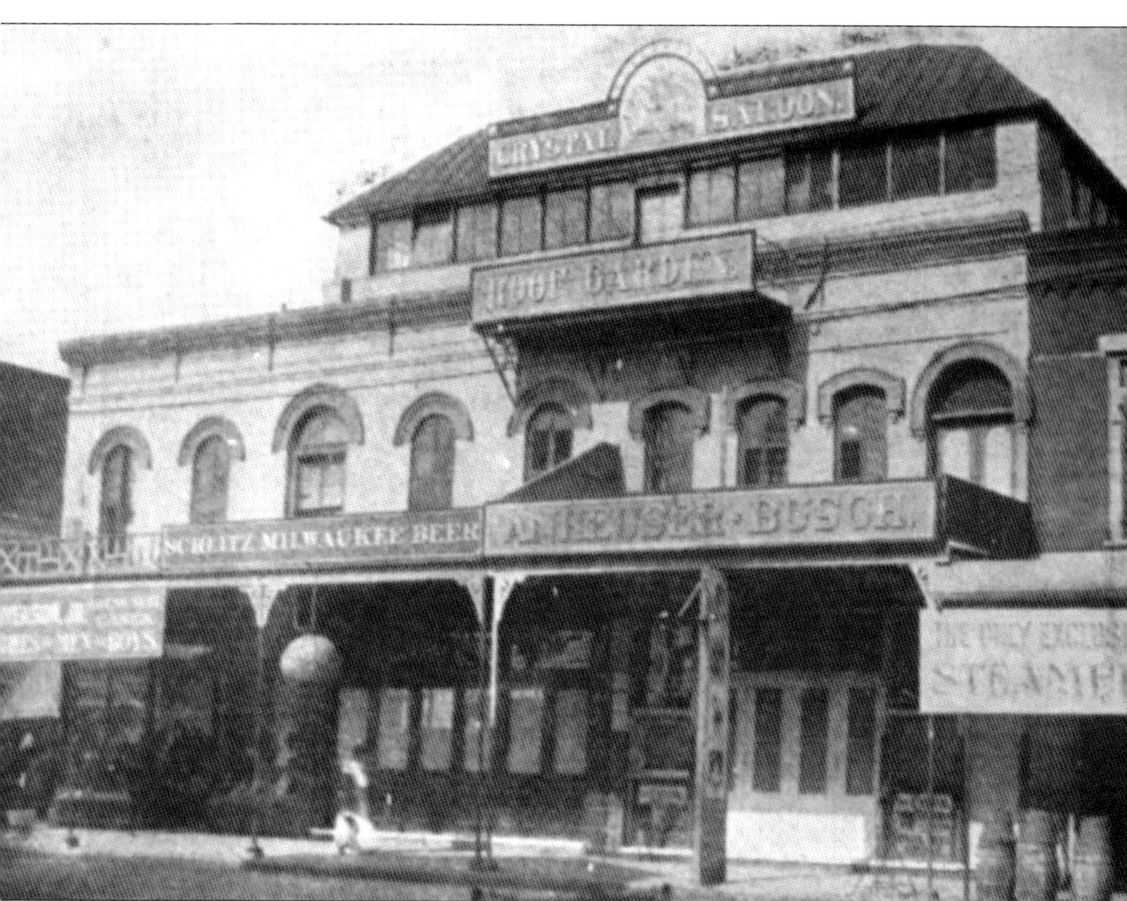

The Crystal Saloon was an impressively large bar with a roof garden located at 135 West Bay Street. The photograph from 1904 shows the Crystal Saloon with various advertisements for Anheuser-Busch and Schlitz beer. (Courtesy of Library of Congress.)

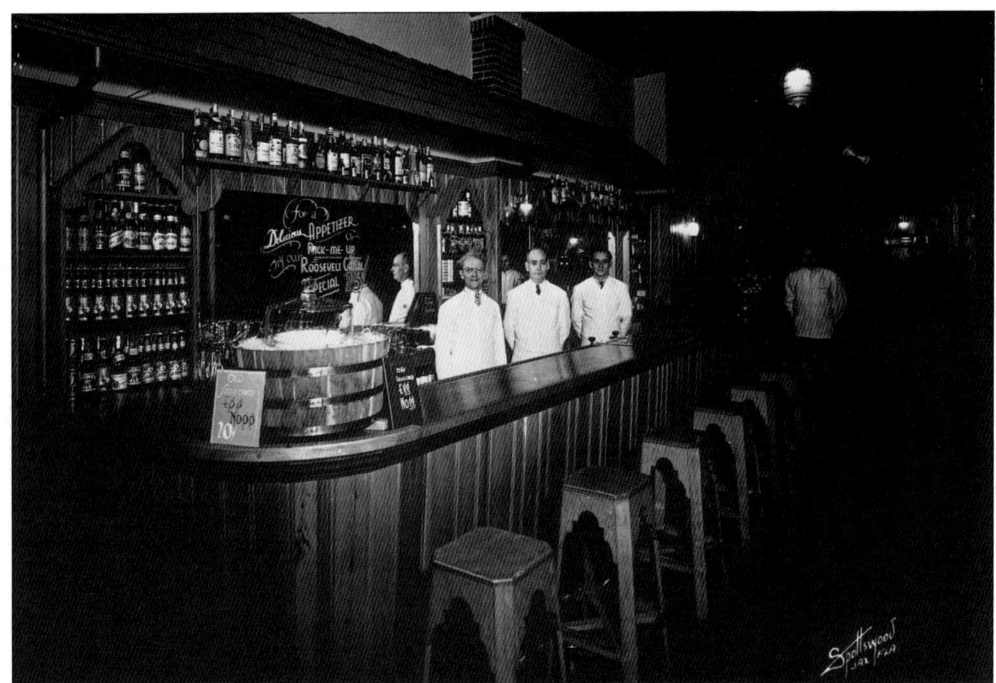

The Seminole Hotel opened in 1909 and was located at the corner of Hogan and Forsyth Streets. Like all hotels at the time, there was a bar to accommodate the many guests that came to Jacksonville. The photograph shows the bar at the Seminole Hotel in 1935. To the left of the bartenders is a variety of beers on the wall. (Courtesy of State Archives of Florida.)

Beers and Ales		
On Draught { Schlitz		10c
On Draught { Wagner		10c
Krueger's Beer and Ale	Can	15c
Budweiser	Bot.	15c
Schlitz	"	15c
Blue Ribbon	"	15c
Ostner's Ale	"	15c
Ostner's Stout	"	15c
Jax Beer	"	10c
Old Union	"	10c
Wagner Beer	"	10c
Old South Beer	"	10c
Ballantine Ale	Can	15c
Ballantine Ale	Bot.	15c

The menu of the Seminole Hotel bar shows an assortment of beers and ales available. Krueger's Beer and Ale comes from the Gottfried Krueger Brewing Company of Newark, New Jersey. Ostner's Ale and Ostner's Stout come from the Jax Brewing Company and are named after its founder, William Ostner. The cost of 15¢ in 1935 is equivalent to $3.52 in 2025. (Courtesy of University of North Florida.)

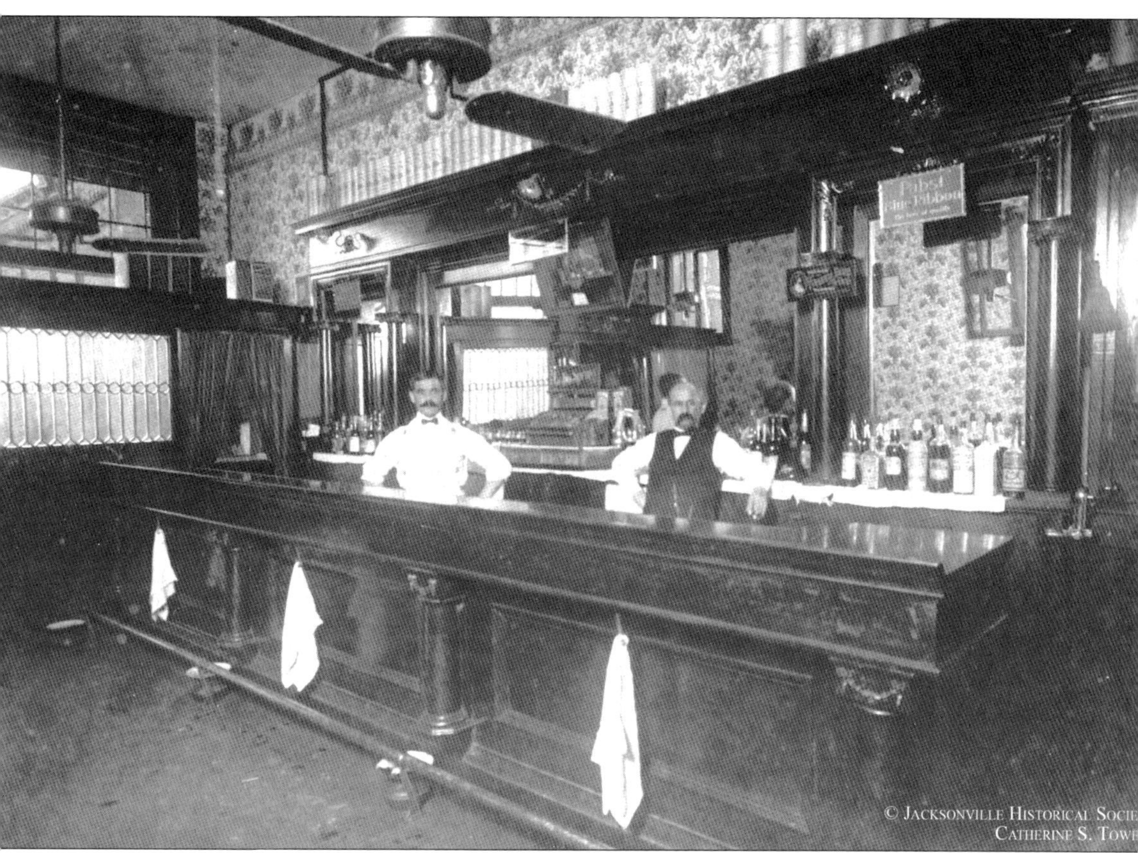

The Onyx Rail Bar Cocktail Lounge was founded in 1899 on Bay Street by German immigrants and closed in 1971. The bar rail is said to have been carved from onyx stone. According to a sign that once hung above the entrance, the Onyx Rail Bar was once the oldest bar in the South. This photograph of the Onyx Rail Bar Cocktail Lounge on West Bay Street in the early 1900s includes a Pabst Blue Ribbon sign hanging above the bartenders. (Courtesy of Jacksonville Historical Society.)

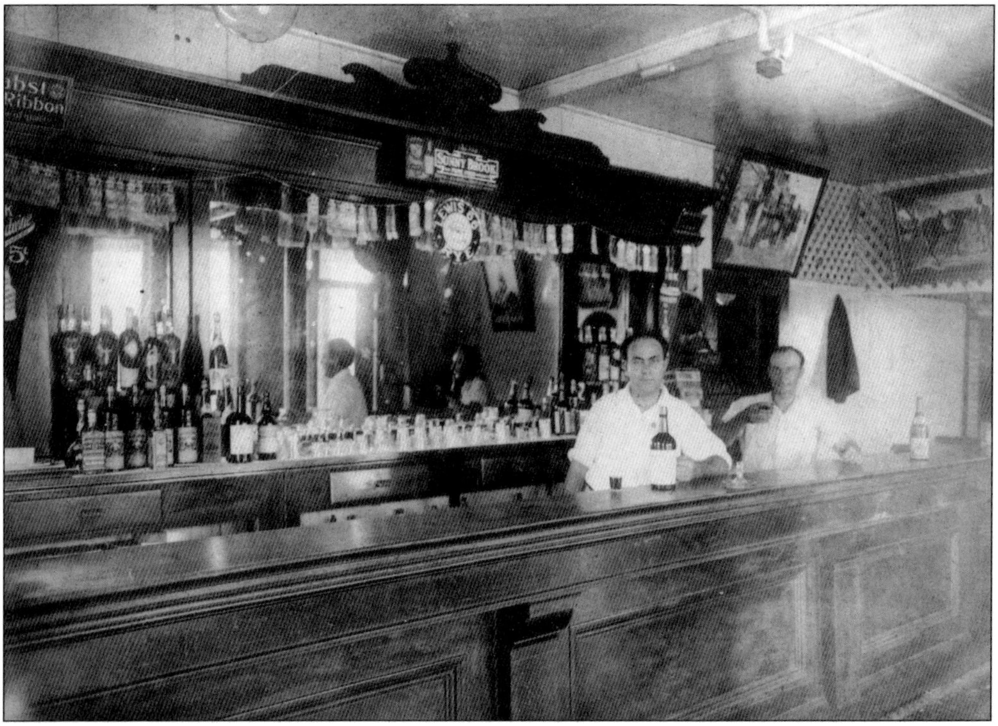

Two bartenders pose at Frank Floyd's Saloon in Mayport around 1910. Frank Floyd was the owner of the saloon as well as the Old Mayport Boarding House. Floyd was known in Mayport as Capt. Frank Floyd and was a popular merchant. Floyd was also a pilot commissioner from the late 1890s to the early 1900s. Signs above the bartenders are for Pabst Blue Ribbon, Sunny Brook whiskey, and Lewis 66 Rye whiskey. (Courtesy of Beaches Museum.)

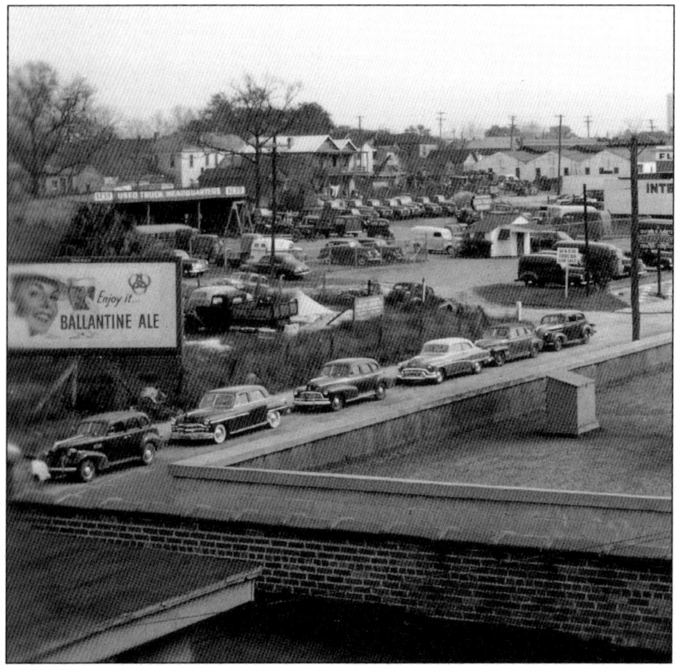

The P. Ballantine and Sons Brewing Company was founded in 1840 by Peter Ballantine in New Jersey. The brewery was notable for brewing ale and becoming the third largest in the United States by the 1950s. P. Ballantine and Sons Brewing Company was once a tenant at a warehouse on Roselle Street in the present-day CoRK Arts District. This photograph shows a Ballantine Ale billboard near Myrtle Avenue in Jacksonville in the 1950s. (Courtesy of Public Library of America.)

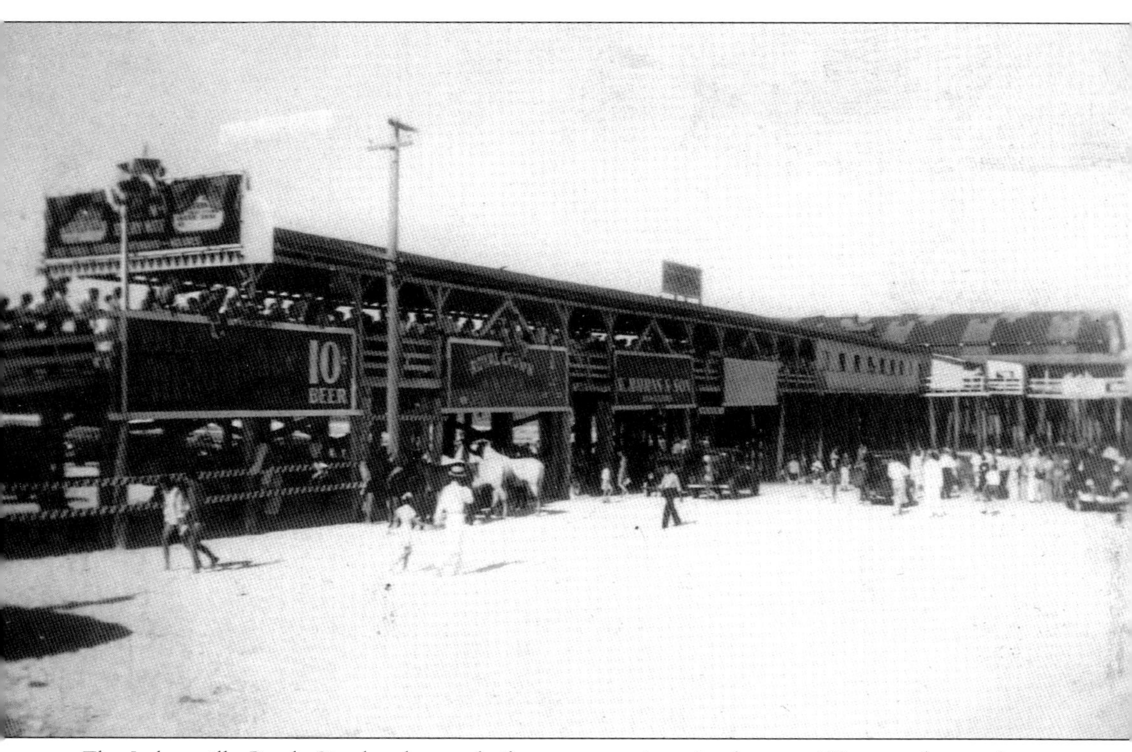

The Jacksonville Beach Pier has been rebuilt numerous times in the past 100 years due to damage from tropical storms and hurricanes. The photograph shows the pier in the 1930s adorned with many advertisements. One such advertisement is for Old Milwaukee Beer, priced at 10¢ in 1935 (adjusted for inflation, about $2.30 in 2025). Old Milwaukee Beer was a brand of American lager owned by the Pabst Brewing Company. (Courtesy of Beaches Museum.)

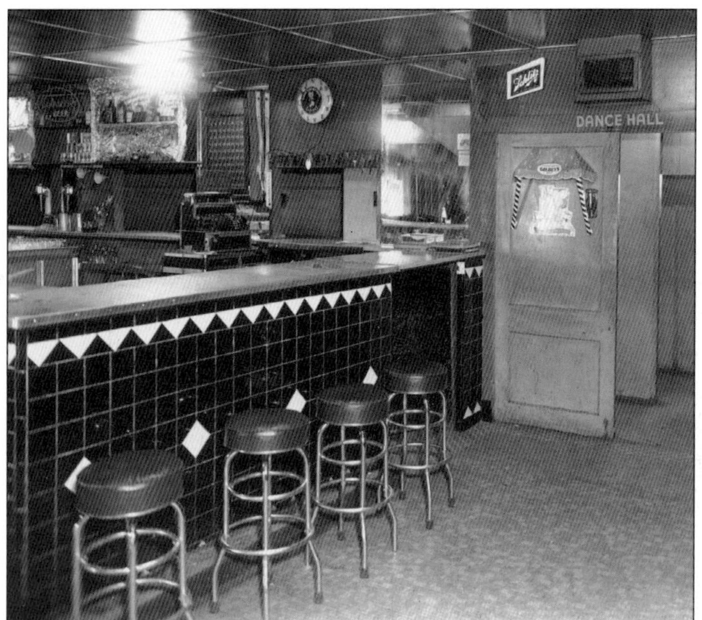

The Two Spot was a club that was opened in 1940 by James "Charlie Edd" Craddock at Forty-Fifth Street and Moncrief Road. The Two Spot changed its name to the Palms Ballroom after the death of Craddock in 1957. In 1967, the club was demolished, and an apartment complex was built on the former site. The photograph shows the bar at the Two Spot featuring a Schlitz sign near the upper right. (Courtesy of State Archives of Florida.)

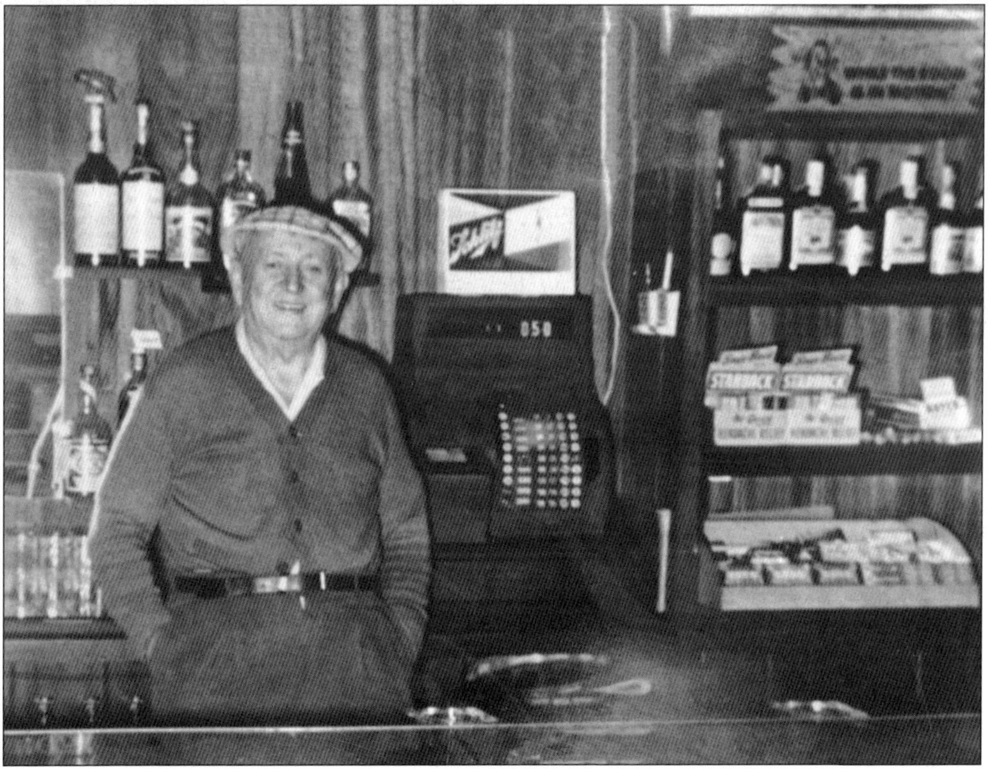

Peter Jensen opened the Jensen Market at present-day Neptune Beach in the 1920s. Jensen sold bootleg liquor from his store during Prohibition. When Prohibition ended in 1933, Jensen applied for a liquor license to open Pete's Bar where his former market once stood. Pete's Bar was the first bar to open in Duval County after Prohibition ended in 1933. The photograph shows Pete Jensen at his bar around 1950. (Courtesy of Beaches Museum.)

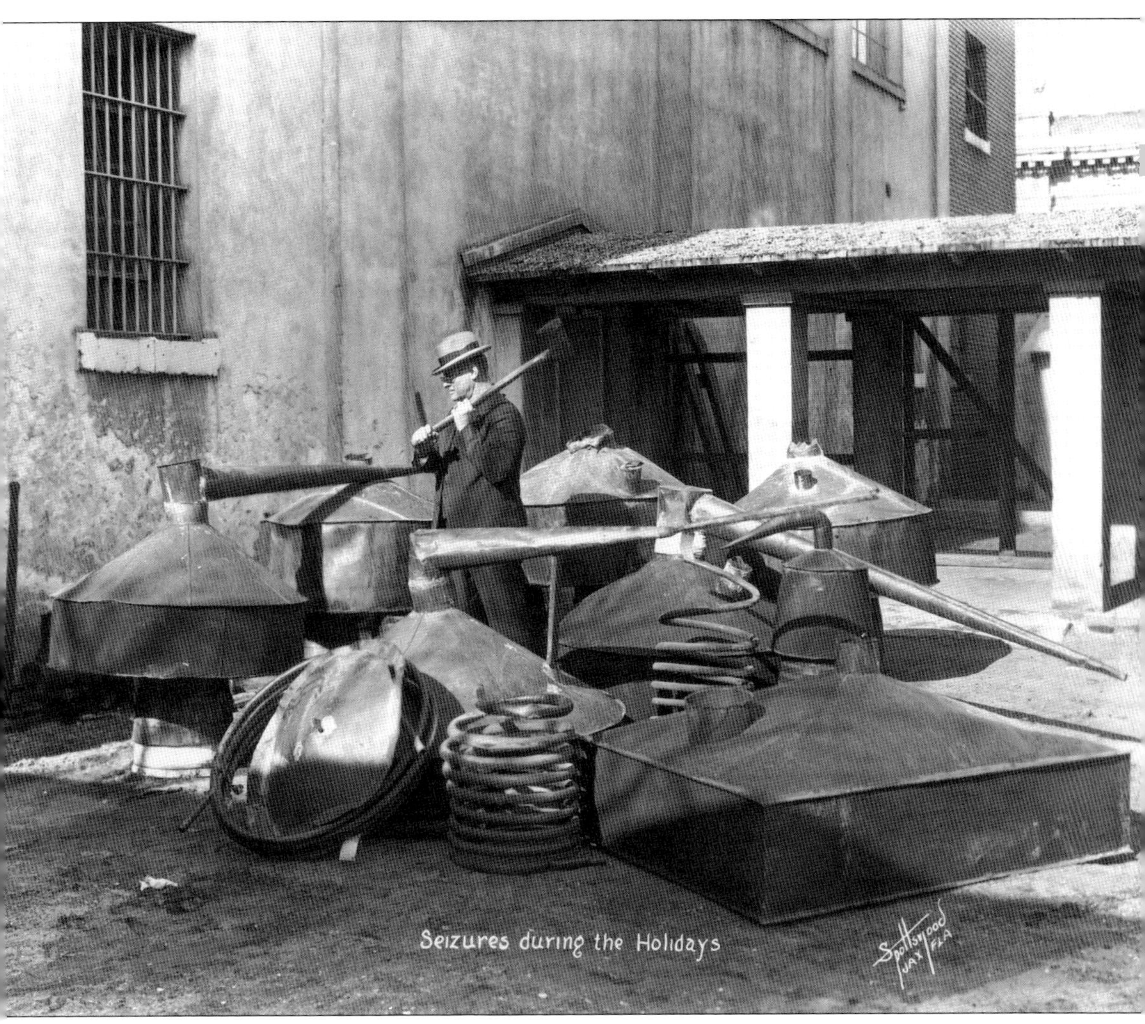

The overall purpose of Prohibition was to reduce or eliminate the supposed immoral aspects of society that were blamed on alcohol consumption. The 18th Amendment prohibited the manufacture, sale, or transportation of intoxicating liquor, including beer. The amendment was proposed by the US Congress in December 1917 and was ratified by the required number of states in January 1919. The Volstead Act, officially called the National Prohibition Act, was enacted on January 16, 1920, to provide guidelines on how to enforce the 18th Amendment. The act was named after Andrew Volstead, who managed the act's legislation on the House Judiciary Committee. Prohibition began on January 17, 1920. Breweries could brew near beer, which is beer that cannot have any more than half of one percent (0.5 percent) alcohol by volume, diversify into other forms of business unrelated to alcohol, or close. This photograph shows an officer of the Jacksonville Sheriff's Office breaking up a distillery in the 1920s as part of enforcing the 18th Amendment. (Courtesy of Jacksonville Public Library.)

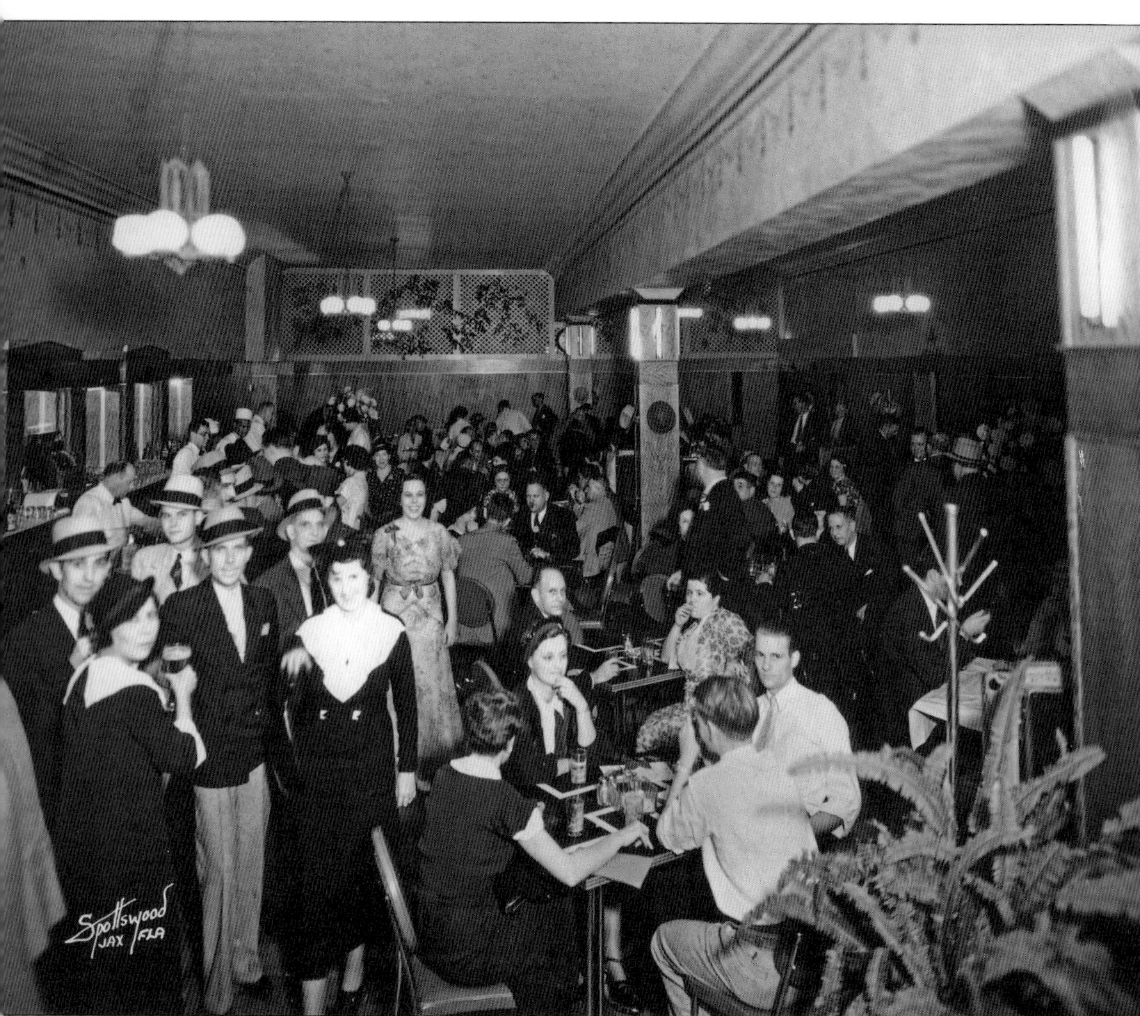

Historian Michael Lerner says that the unintended consequences of Prohibition's failures led to the elimination of jobs, a decline in profits for restaurants and theaters, and the loss of tax revenues on liquor sales for state and federal government. Prohibition led to an opportunity for organized crime to sell beer and liquor through underground networks that became increasingly more difficult for law enforcement to keep up with. On March 21, 1933, Pres. Franklin D. Roosevelt signed the Cullen-Harrison Act, legalizing the sale and consumption of alcohol and wine with a low-alcohol content of 3.2 percent. On February 20, 1933, the 21st Amendment was proposed in the US Congress to repeal Prohibition. Florida ratified the 21st Amendment on November 14, 1933, and on December 5, the amendment was officially ratified by the requisite number of states. This photograph shows a bar called Jimmy Mains in 1933 with patrons celebrating a long overdue drink after the end of Prohibition. As Stephen King, via Horace M. Derwent of the Overlook Hotel, would say, "Great party isn't it?" (Courtesy of State Archives of Florida.)

Two

Early Brewing and Logistics

Eggenweiler & Co. Brewery was the first brewery in Jacksonville. The advertisement of Eggenweiler & Co.'s Brewery from 1871 highlights lager beer brewed by the brewery. The brewery was located in the LaVilla neighborhood on West Bay Street, but it was only in operation for a short period of time. The brewery was founded by Louis Eggenweiler, born Ludwig Eggenweiler in 1822 in the Kingdom of Württemberg, Germany. (Courtesy of Jacksonville Public Library.)

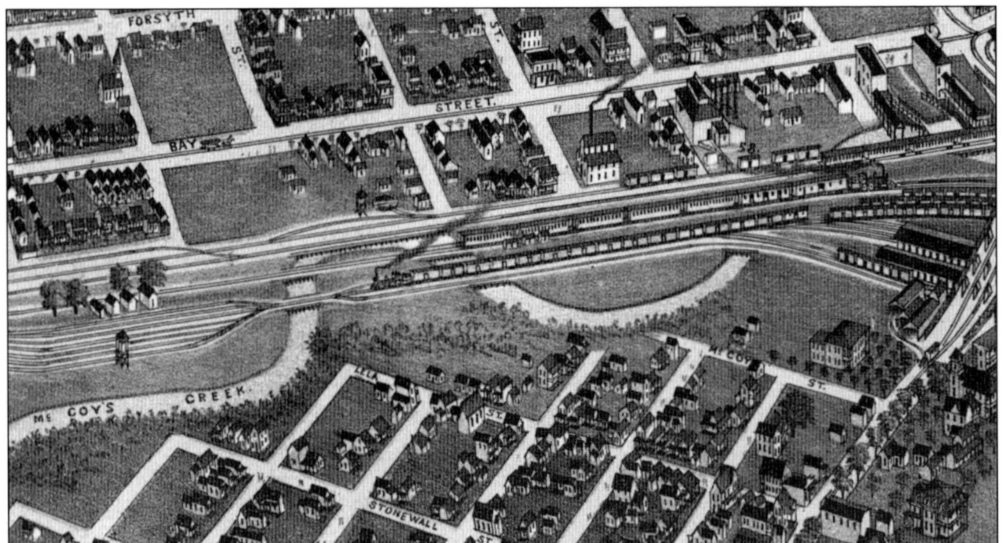

Eggenweiler's brewery was only in operation for a few short years and existed largely because of advances in refrigeration. The Philadelphia-based brewery Bergner & Engel Brewing Company had the resources to utilize the full potential in the logistics of beer and the new advances of refrigeration. This portion of a bird's-eye-view map of Jacksonville from 1893 shows what was Bergner & Engel's Florida depot as the two near-identical buildings in the upper-right corner. (Courtesy of Library of Congress.)

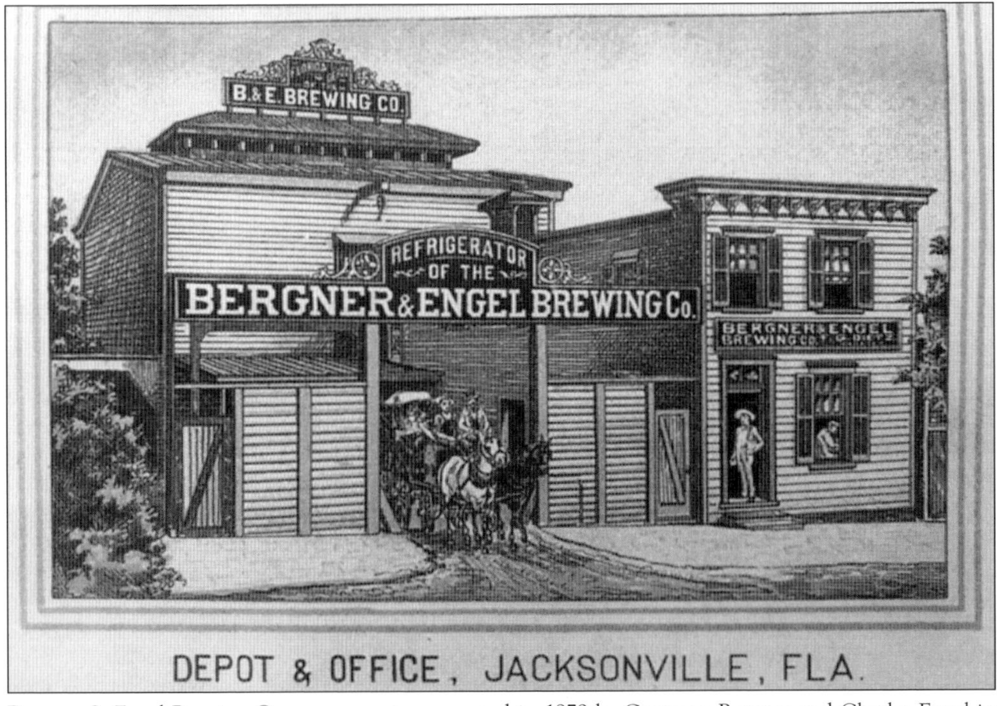

Bergner & Engel Brewing Company was incorporated in 1879 by Gustavus Bergner and Charles Engel in Philadelphia. It became one of the largest breweries at the time with multiple locations. The brewery owned refrigerator train cars for transporting along the Atlantic coast. Refrigeration of beer is necessary because it helps preserve a beer's flavor over large distances. The picture shows the Bergner & Engel Brewing Company's Florida depot in the LaVilla district of Jacksonville. (Courtesy of Library Company of Philadelphia.)

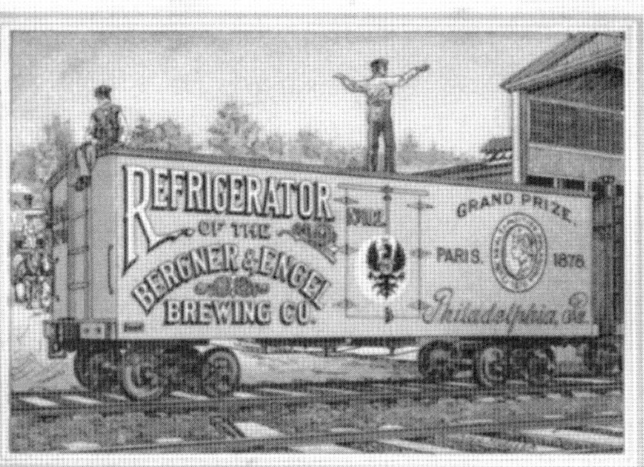

REFRIGERATING CAR FOR THE TRANSPORTATION OF BEER, ALE & PORTER

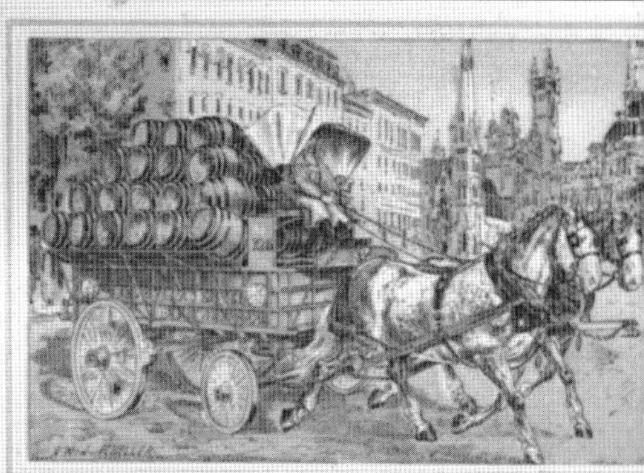

DELIVERY WAGON.

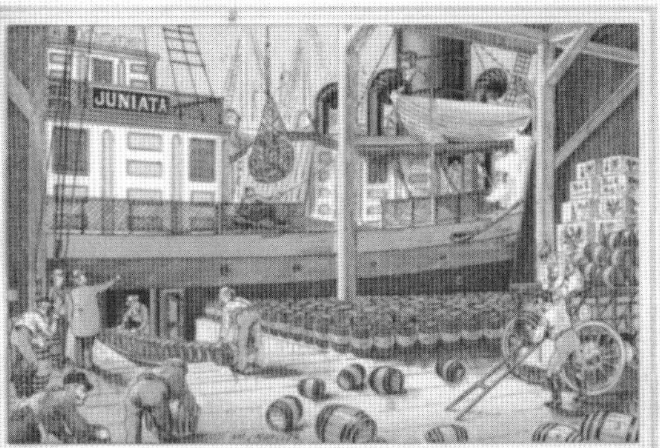

LOADING THE JUNIATA. O.S.S. Co. FOR SAVANNAH. GA.

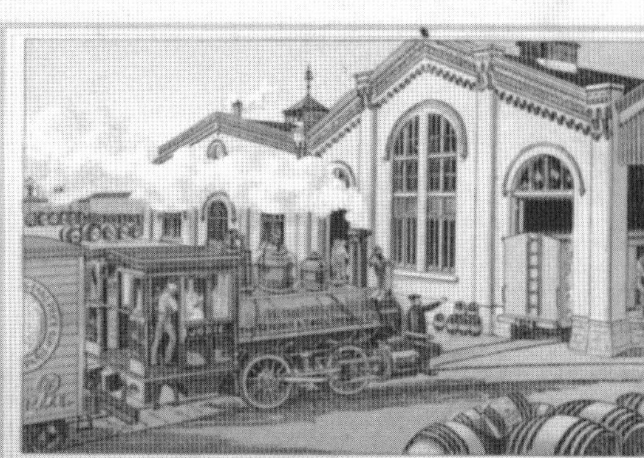

THE FIRST AND ONLY LOCOMOTIVE
OWNED AND OPERATED BY ANY BREWING ESTABLISHMENT IN AMERICA

Charles Engel was born in 1816 in Germany. In 1840, Engel immigrated to Philadelphia, where he began brewing as a partner with Charles Wolf, forming Engel & Wolf's Lager Beer Brewery. Gustavus Bergner was born in 1832 also in Germany. Gustavus's father, Charles Bergner, built a brewery on Seventh Street in Philadelphia where his son learned the trade of brewing. Engel acquired Wolf's shares in the brewery and formed a partnership with brewer Gustavus Bergner in 1872 to form Bergner & Engel Brewing Company. By 1875, it was the third-largest brewery in the United States. The sketches show the logistics of Bergner & Engel Brewing Company beer, including its refrigerated train car, delivery wagons, and transportation via ships and locomotives. (Courtesy of Library Company of Philadelphia.)

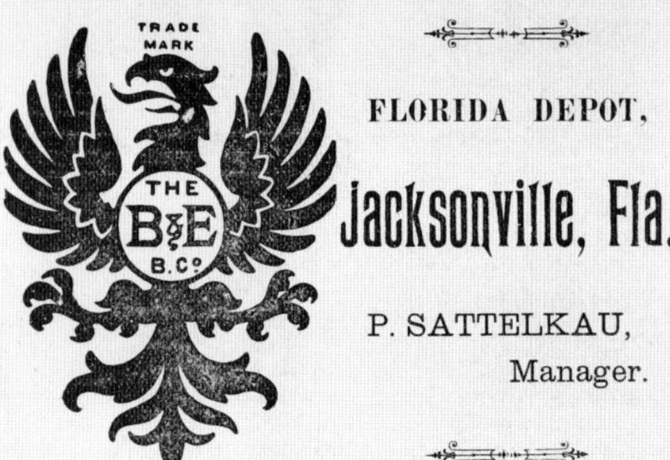

Cold temperatures are needed for lager fermentation as well as for the storing of beer, which would be between three and six months. The late 19th century saw a change in how beer was fermented and stored in warmer places like Florida because of the new technology of ice-making. This advertisement from 1890 shows Bergner & Engel's Florida depot at Jacksonville and its main beer, called Tannhaeuser. (Courtesy of Library of Congress.)

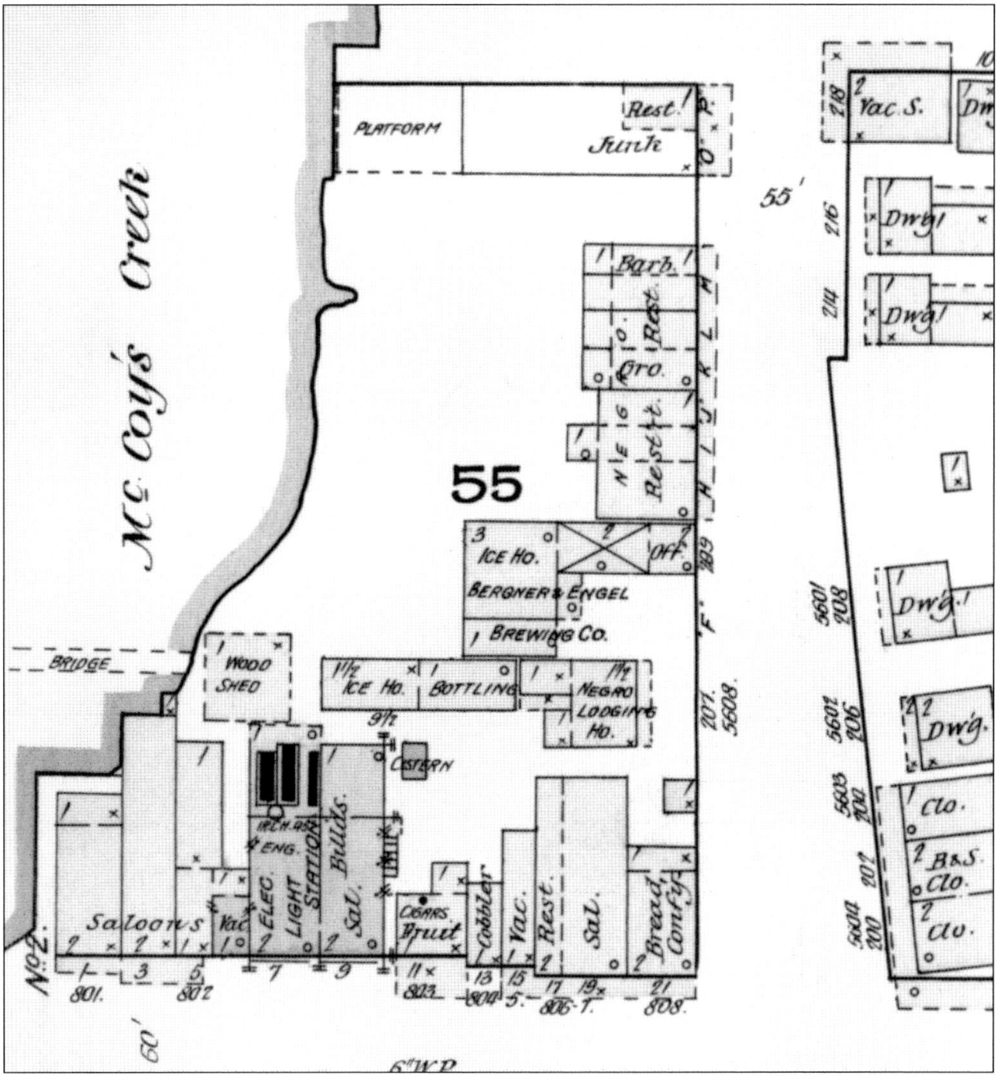

This Sanborn Fire Insurance Company map from 1887 shows Bergner & Engel's Florida depot on McCoys Creek in the center of block 55. One block away is the El Modelo Cigar Factory building, which still stands as of 2024. The Federal Reserve Bank of Atlanta, Jacksonville Branch, occupies the general area where the Bergner & Engel Florida depot was once located. (Courtesy of Library of Congress.)

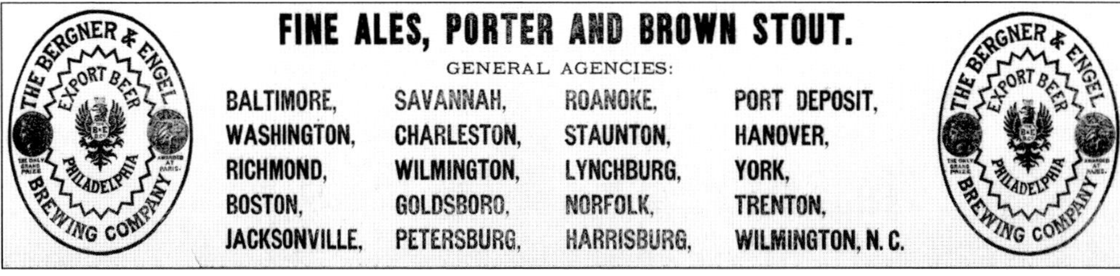

This advertisement from 1888 shows the locations of Bergner & Engel Brewing Company, including its Jacksonville location. A fire burned down its Florida depot, and a new brick structure was built in 1891. The Jos. Zapf Company occupied the building in the late 1890s. (Courtesy of *Philadelphia Times*.)

The Henry Mason Company was a wholesale dealer in beer, wine, and whiskey, first opening in 1882 at 115 West Bay Street. This advertisement from 1890 shows the dealer having beer from Milwaukee, Bergner & Engel, and Cook Brewing Company. (Courtesy of Library of Congress.)

The advertisement shows Kornahrens' Steam Bottling Works being the agent for F.W. Cook Brewing Company of Evansville, Indiana, in Jacksonville. Kornahrens' Steam Bottling Works was located at the Meyer & Muller building on East Bay Street. The owners of Meyer & Muller were Claus Meyer and Gustav Muller, both from Germany. (Courtesy of Library of Congress.)

Gustav Muller was born on February 10, 1874, in Jacksonville to Janey and Gustav Muller. His father was born Gustav Müller in 1849 in Germany and immigrated to the United States in the 1860s. His father was a successful businessman from the firm Meyer & Muller. Gustav emulated his father's successes as a businessman by becoming a commissioner in Jacksonville and owning the Floridian Hotel, Hotel Burbridge, and a beer bottling business in Jacksonville. (Courtesy of Jacksonville Historical Society.)

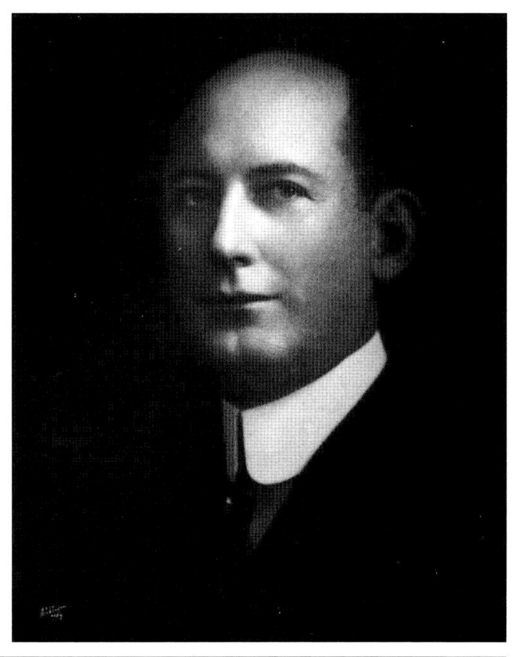

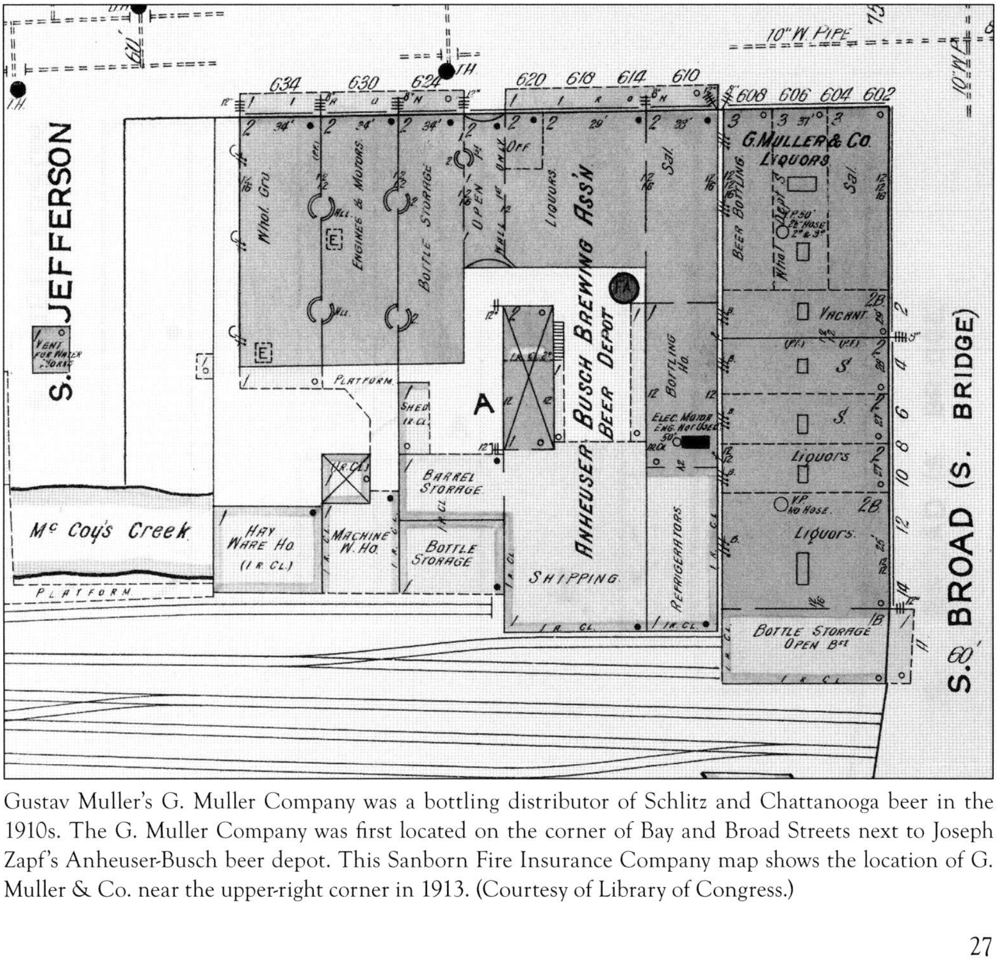

Gustav Muller's G. Muller Company was a bottling distributor of Schlitz and Chattanooga beer in the 1910s. The G. Muller Company was first located on the corner of Bay and Broad Streets next to Joseph Zapf's Anheuser-Busch beer depot. This Sanborn Fire Insurance Company map shows the location of G. Muller & Co. near the upper-right corner in 1913. (Courtesy of Library of Congress.)

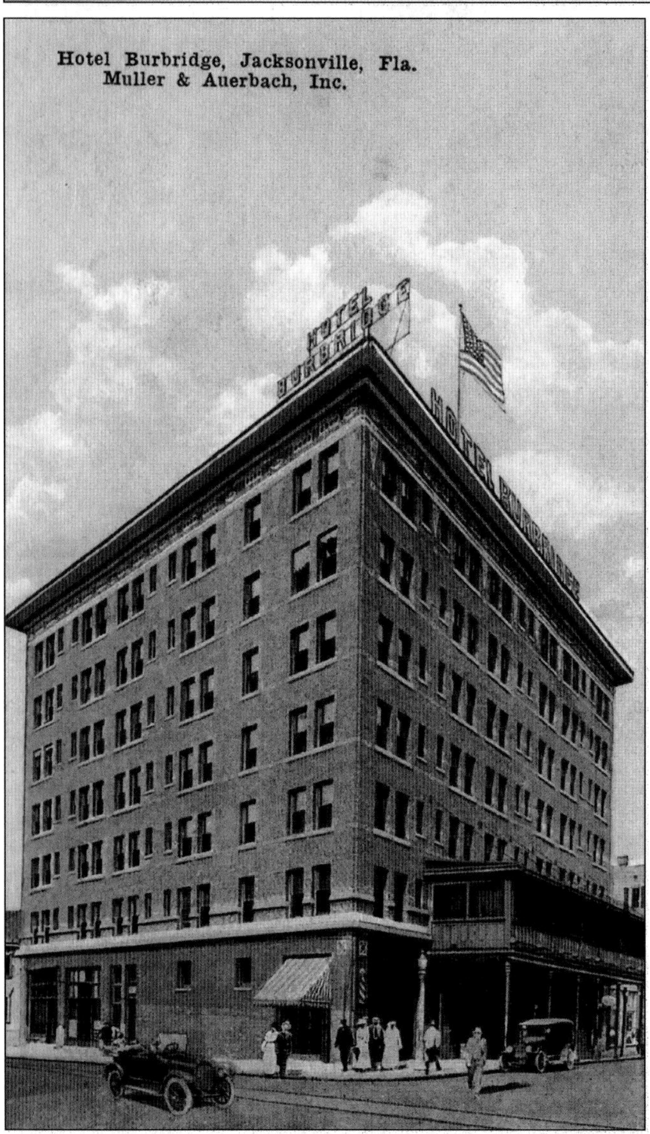

In 1914, the G. Muller Company relocated to a warehouse at 1530 Enterprise Street, the former name of Beaver Street. This advertisement from the late 1910s shows the beer that the G. Muller Company distributed. In faded white, the words "Agents for Chattanooga Beer and Schlitz" can still be seen on the G. Muller Company's Enterprise Street building at the present-day Myrtle Avenue Brewing Company. (Courtesy of Jacksonville Public Library.)

The Hotel Burbridge opened in 1911 at West Forsyth Street and Clay Street. William Burbridge commissioned architect Henry Klutho to design the hotel with 175 rooms and a lobby decorated with hunting trophies. In 1915, Gustav Muller became associated with the hotel as its manager. In the 1940s, the hotel was renamed the Hotel Floridan. In 1977, the hotel closed, and it was demolished in 1981. (Courtesy of Jacksonville Historical Society.)

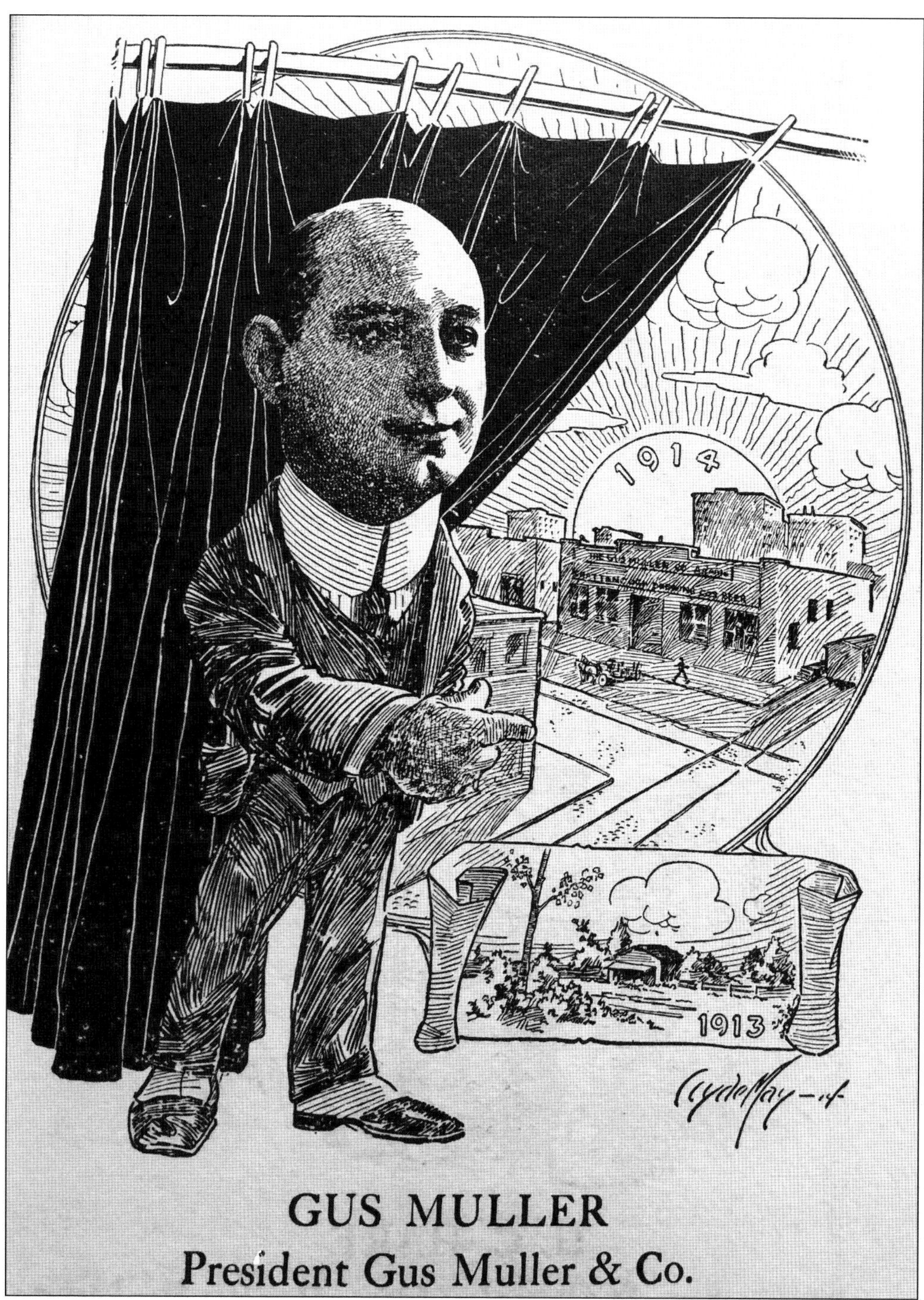

GUS MULLER
President Gus Muller & Co.

Muller's success in the brewing industry was not only confined to Jacksonville but also extended to Miami, where he was a manager at the Hotel McCallister. In 1932, Muller announced plans to establish a brewery in Miami called the Gustav Muller Brewing Company whenever all laws were in place to allow it after Prohibition officially ended. Despite Muller's ambitious plans and necessary funds to establish his brewery right after Prohibition, it never came to fruition. (Courtesy of Jacksonville Public Library.)

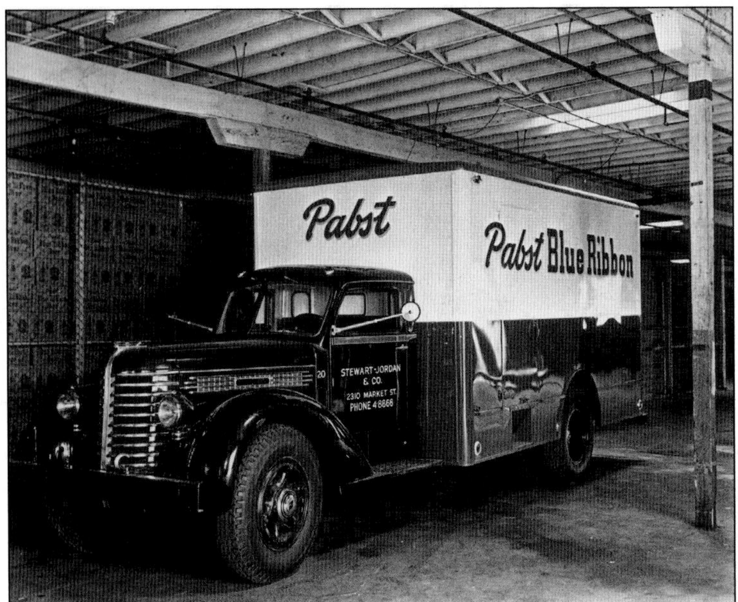

Pabst Blue Ribbon began making an appearance in Jacksonville by the early 1900s with the Charles Blum Company as its distributor. Stewart-Jordan & Co. was a later distributor of Pabst Blue Ribbon in Jacksonville. The photograph shows a Stewart-Jordan & Co. delivery truck with "Pabst Blue Ribbon" on its side in Jacksonville in 1949. (Courtesy of State Archives of Florida.)

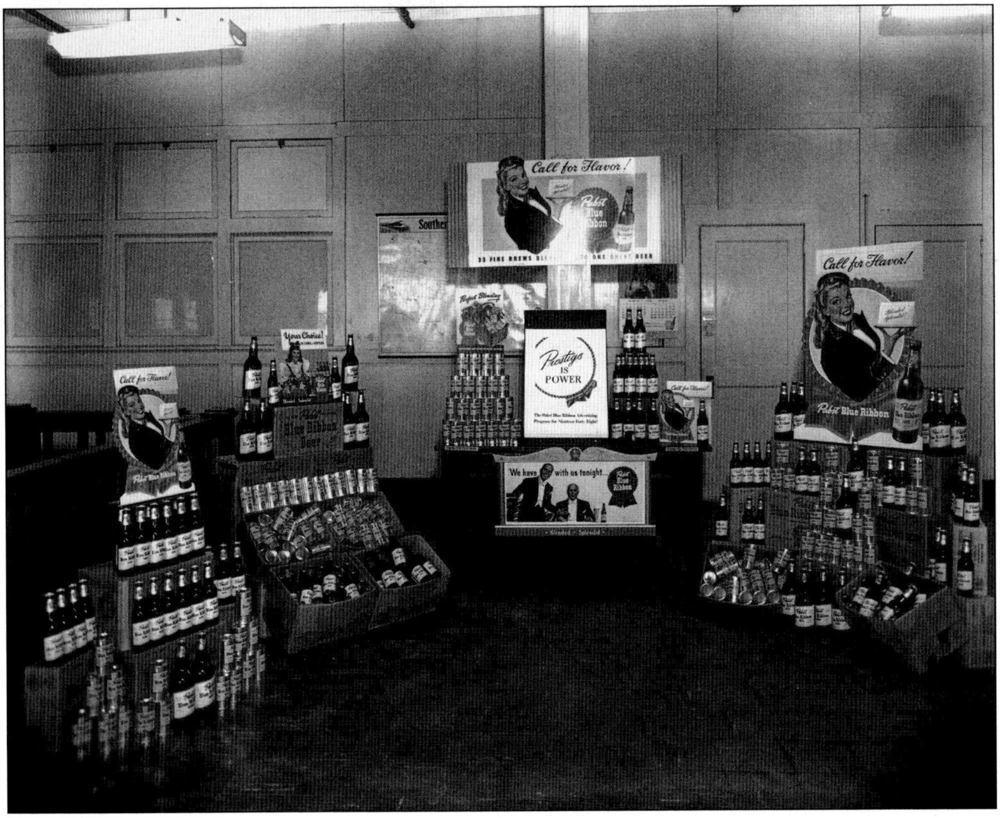

One notable brand by Pabst Brewing Company was Best's Select lager, which was renamed Pabst Blue Ribbon in 1893. Pabst Blue Ribbon beer was brewed at its Milwaukee brewery from 1844 to 1996. MillerCoors took over the brewing operations of Pabst Blue Ribbon in 1999. The photograph shows a Pabst Blue Ribbon beer display at a grocery store in Jacksonville in 1948. (Courtesy of State Archives of Florida.)

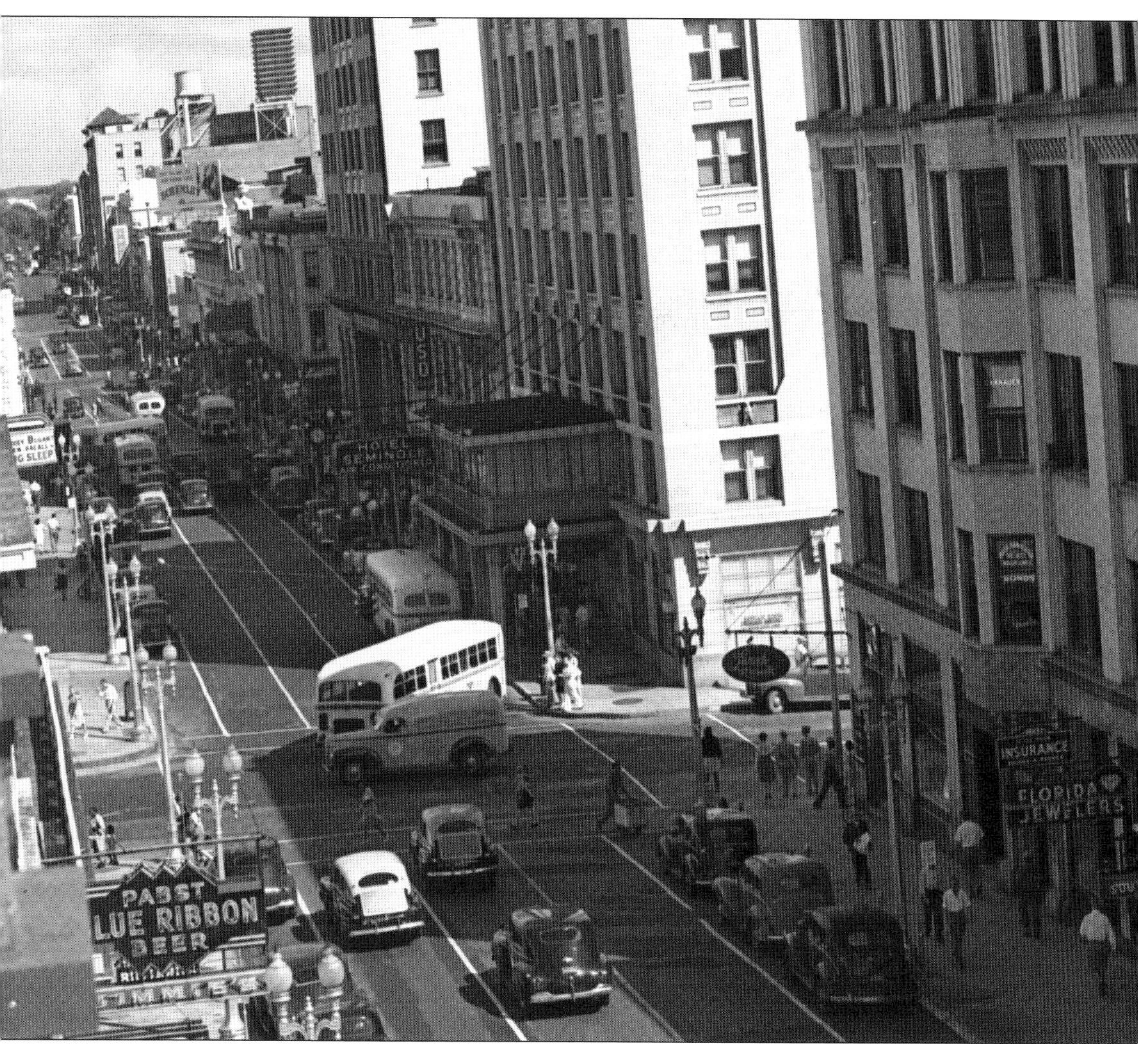

The photograph shows Hogan Street in downtown Jacksonville with a Pabst Blue Ribbon sign in the lower left. The Seminole Hotel can be seen in the center with the balcony jutting out on the second floor. (Courtesy of State Archives of Florida.)

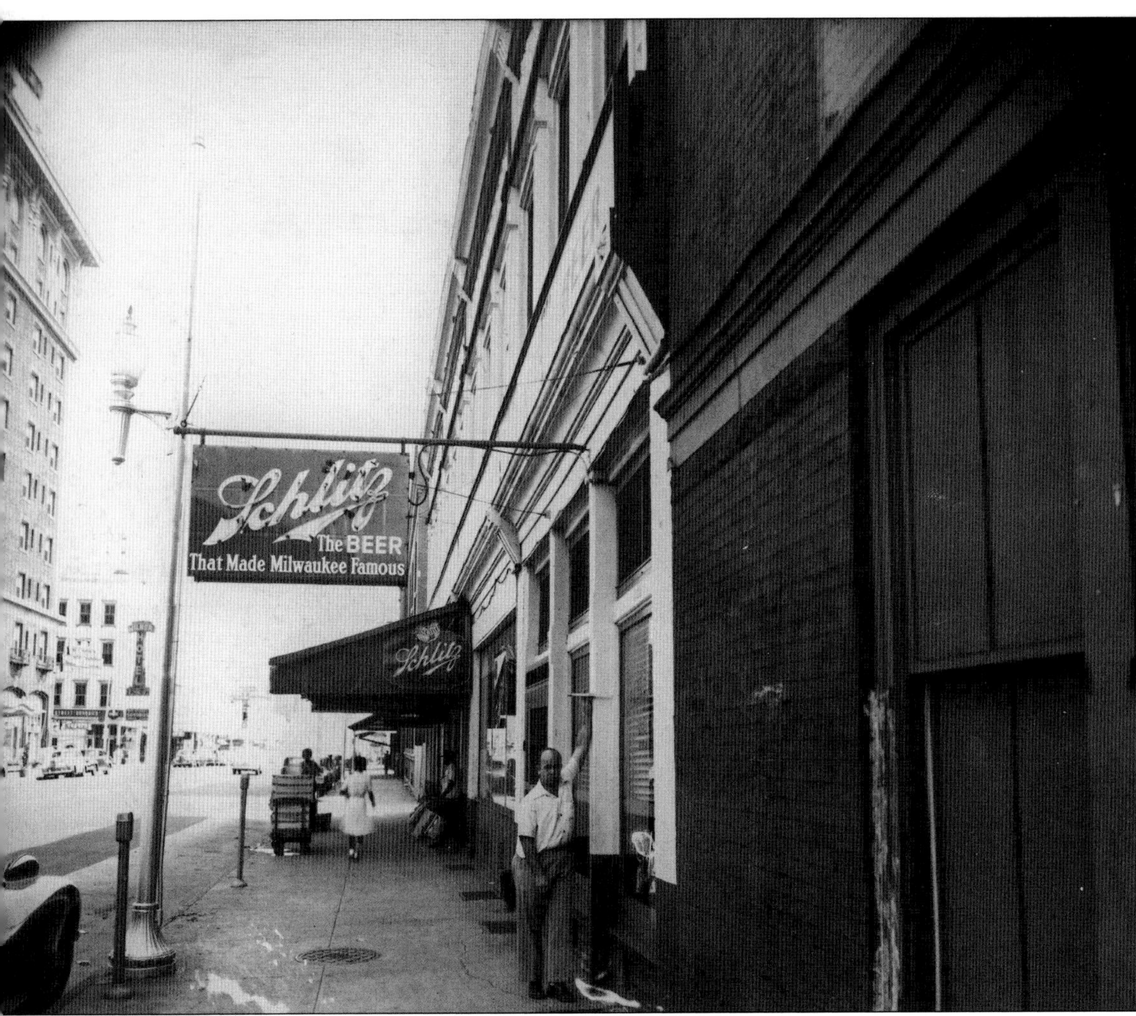

Schlitz was a Milwaukee beer manufactured by the Joseph Schlitz Brewing Company. Schlitz was once a popular beer in the mid-20th century, considered one of the top brands along with Anheuser-Busch and Pabst Blue Ribbon. The photograph shows a Schlitz sign on the Tyler & Sons building at 324 West Bay Street in downtown Jacksonville in 1948. (Courtesy of State Archives of Florida.)

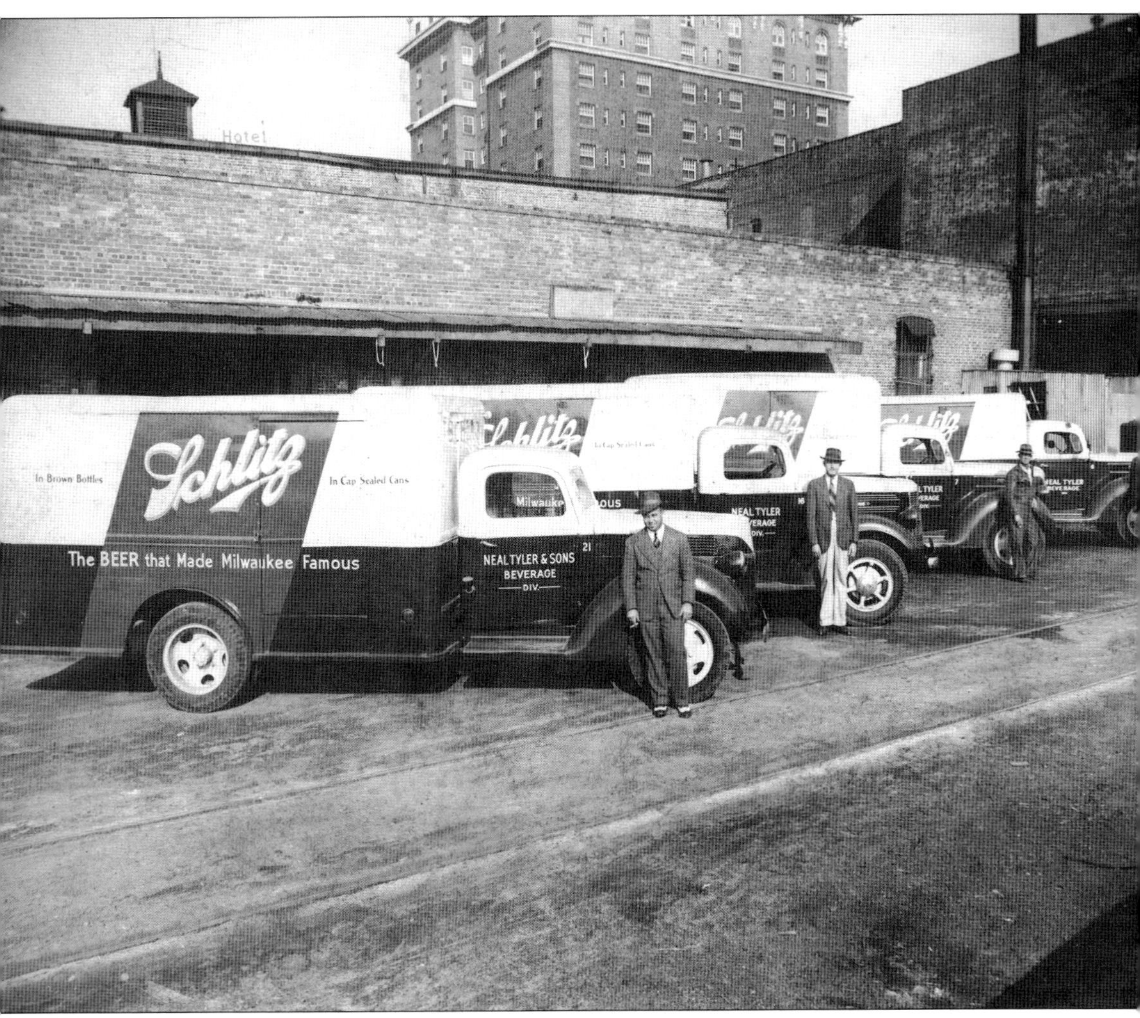

Neal Tyler & Sons delivery trucks are adorned with the Schlitz logo around 1950. Schlitz continued to remain a favorite beer for Americans in the 1950s and 1960s. In the 1970s, Schlitz altered its beer to lower costs in production but was not well received by consumers. In 1976, a disastrous ad campaign dubbed the "Drink Schlitz or I'll kill you" advertisement furthered the decline of Schlitz. (Courtesy of Jacksonville Historical Society.)

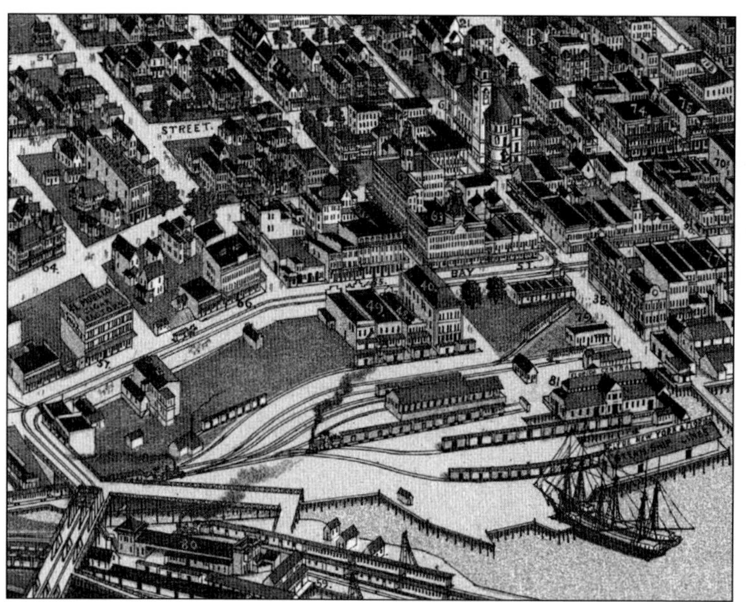

Robert Welborn Simms founded the Robert W. Simms Company in Jacksonville as an importer of mineral spring water, wine, liquor, and beer. The company was once a distributor of Schlitz and Milwaukee beer in the early 1900s. This portion of Augustus Koch's 1893 map of Florida shows the Robert W. Simms Company, No. 49 in the center. On the left side of the map is El Modelo Cigar Factory. (Courtesy of Library of Congress.)

The Bartholomay Brewing Company was founded in 1874 by Henry Bartholomay in Rochester, New York. The advertisement from 1913 shows the Robert W. Simms Co. advertising Bartholomay's Rochester Beer. After retiring in 1916, Simms went into the real estate business and acquired the Andrew Jackson Hotel, Hotel Albert, and other properties in the area. (Courtesy of Jacksonville Public Library.)

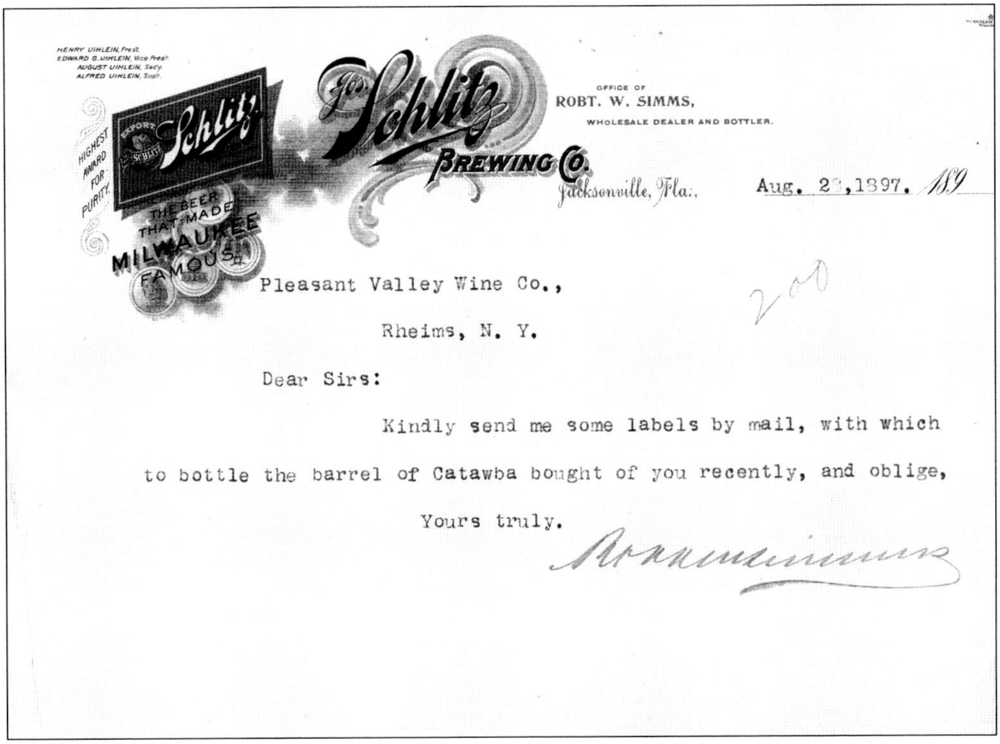

HENRY UIHLEIN, Pres't.
EDWARD G. UIHLEIN, Vice Pres't.
AUGUST UIHLEIN, Sec'y.
ALFRED UIHLEIN, Sup't.

Jos. Schlitz Brewing Co.
Jacksonville, Fla.,

OFFICE OF
ROBT. W. SIMMS,
WHOLESALE DEALER AND BOTTLER.

Aug. 23, 1897. 189

Pleasant Valley Wine Co.,

Rheims, N. Y.

Dear Sirs:

Kindly send me some labels by mail, with which
to bottle the barrel of Catawba bought of you recently, and oblige,

Yours truly.

This is a letter to Pleasant Valley Wine Company written on a Robt. W. Simms letterhead in 1897. (Courtesy of Jacksonville Historical Society.)

W.F. Seeba was a mail-order liquor house featuring a wide assortment of liquor and beer in Jacksonville. Seeba was also the southern agent for Piel Brothers Brewery East New York Brewery. The brewery was founded in 1883 by Gottfried Piel, Michael Piel, and Wilhelm Piel. The advertisement from 1917 shows Seeba's business on Forsyth Street. (Courtesy of *Columbia Record*.)

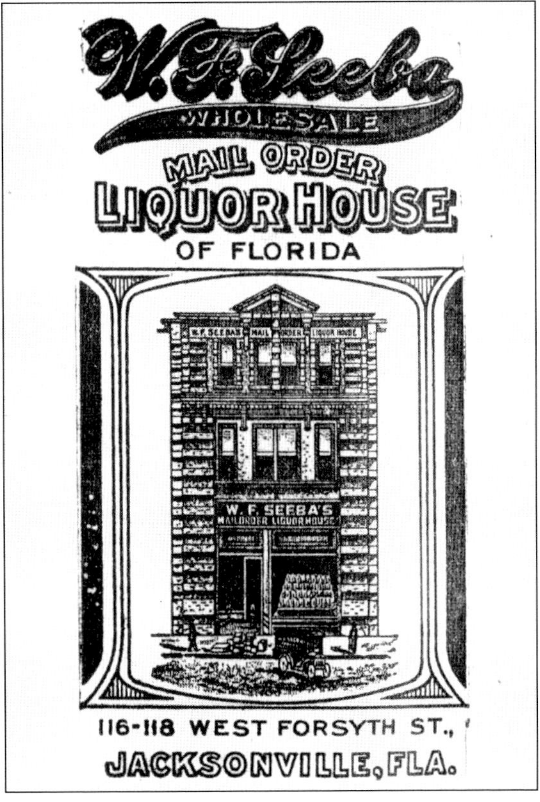

HURNER BROS.

PHONE 3934

254-256 RIVERSIDE AVE.

JACKSONVILLE, FLORIDA

We carry constantly in stock the following brands of Bottled Beers, and are prepared to deliver them off the ice promptly during the legal hours of sale in any quantity from **TWO Bottles up:**

	Per Doz.
BALTIMORE EXTRA PALE	$ .90
Fehr's Extra Pale	1.00
Empire Export	1.00
Cook's Pilsener	1.00
PERFECT BREW (Monumental Brewing Co.'s Baltimore Beer)	1.50
Budweiser	1.50
Rienzi, Rochester, N. Y., Beer	1.50
Piel's Dortmunder	1.50
Pabst Blue Ribbon	1.50
Schlitz, in Brown Bottles	1.50
Bass (White Label) Ale and Porter ....Nips	1.50

Promising first-class service, we solicit your patronage.

Hurner Brothers

This Hurner Bros. advertisement from 1913 showcases their inventory of beer to consumers. Fehr's Extra Pale was brewed by the Fehr Brewing Company in Louisville, Kentucky. (Courtesy of Jacksonville Public Library.)

Around 1895, German immigrant Charles Blum and his brother Jacob established a wholesale liquor business called Charles Blum & Company. It was located on West Bay Street, where Blum had a saloon and liquor dealer. The business became known for its whiskey, notably Sylvan Glen and Blum's Monogram, which were packaged in ceramic jugs. (Courtesy of Jacksonville Public Library.)

This invoice from Charles Blum & Company is dated September 2, 1908. Charles Blum & Company was also the main distributor of Pabst Brewing Company in Jacksonville in the early 1900s. The logo of Pabst Brewing Company, seen on the invoice on the left side, has a letter B in the center representing its former name, Best Brewing Company. (Courtesy of Jacksonville Historically Society.)

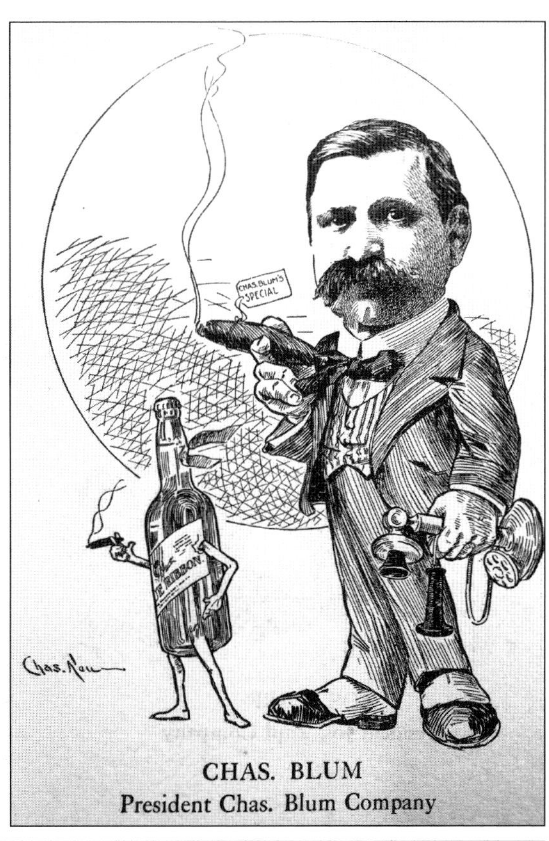

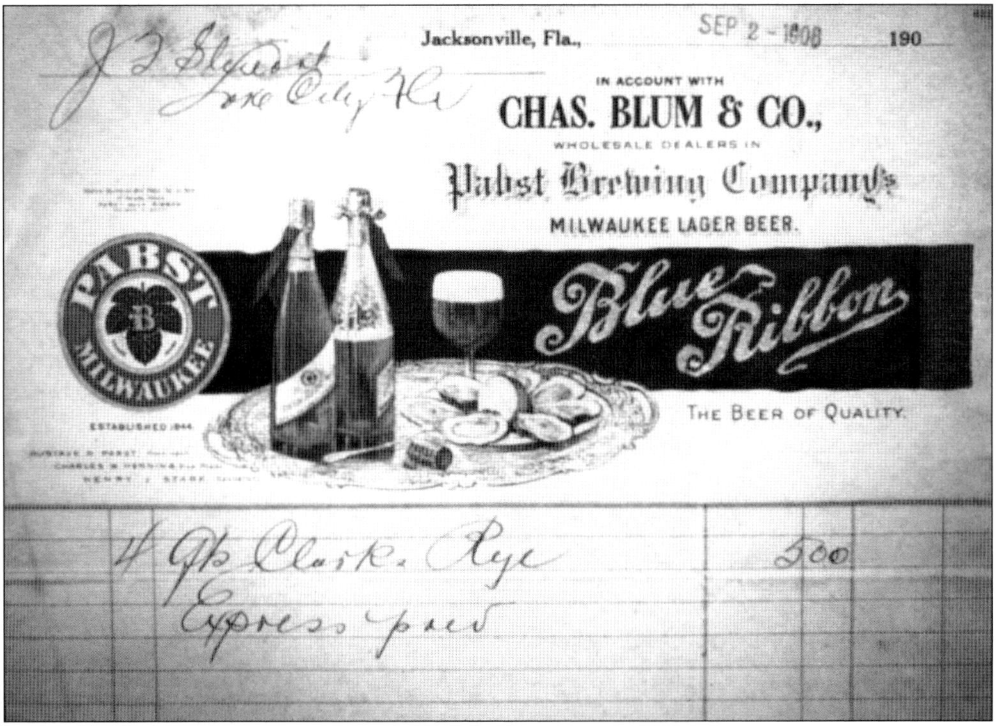

CHAS. BLUM
President Chas. Blum Company

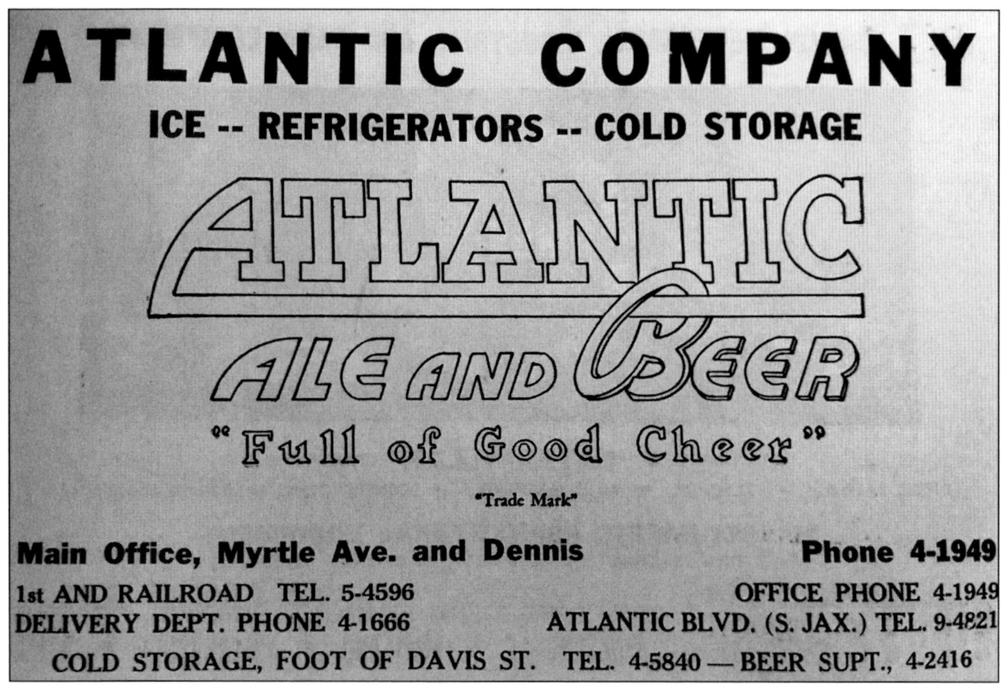

The advertisement for the Atlantic Company from 1950 showcases its cold storage and beer at Myrtle Avenue and Dennis Street. The Atlantic Company was based out of Atlanta and was the largest regional brewery in the South in the 1940s. (Courtesy of Jacksonville Public Library.)

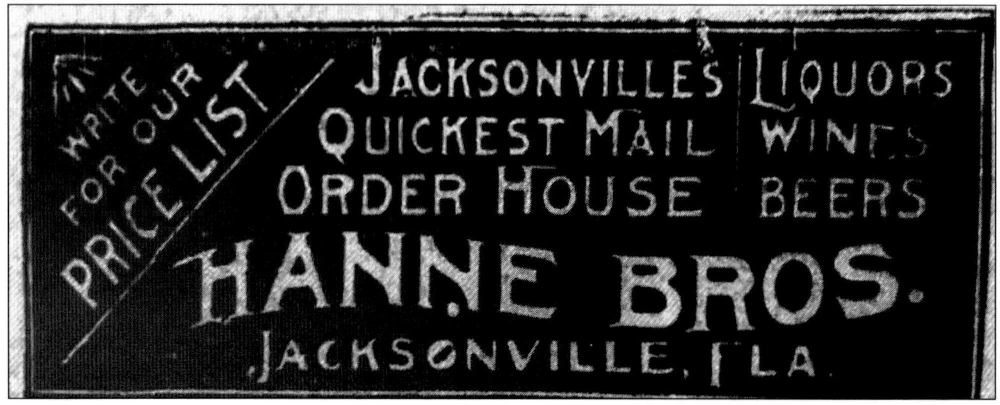

Hanne Bros. was established in 1889 on Adams Street by German immigrants Louis Hanne and Frederick "Harry" Hanne. It was a distributor and bottling plant of liquor and beer. Hanne Bros. was the authorized distributor of William J. Lemp Brewing Company of St. Louis. The ad from 1908 features the logo of Hanne Bros. and their products for mail order. (Courtesy of *Montgomery Times*.)

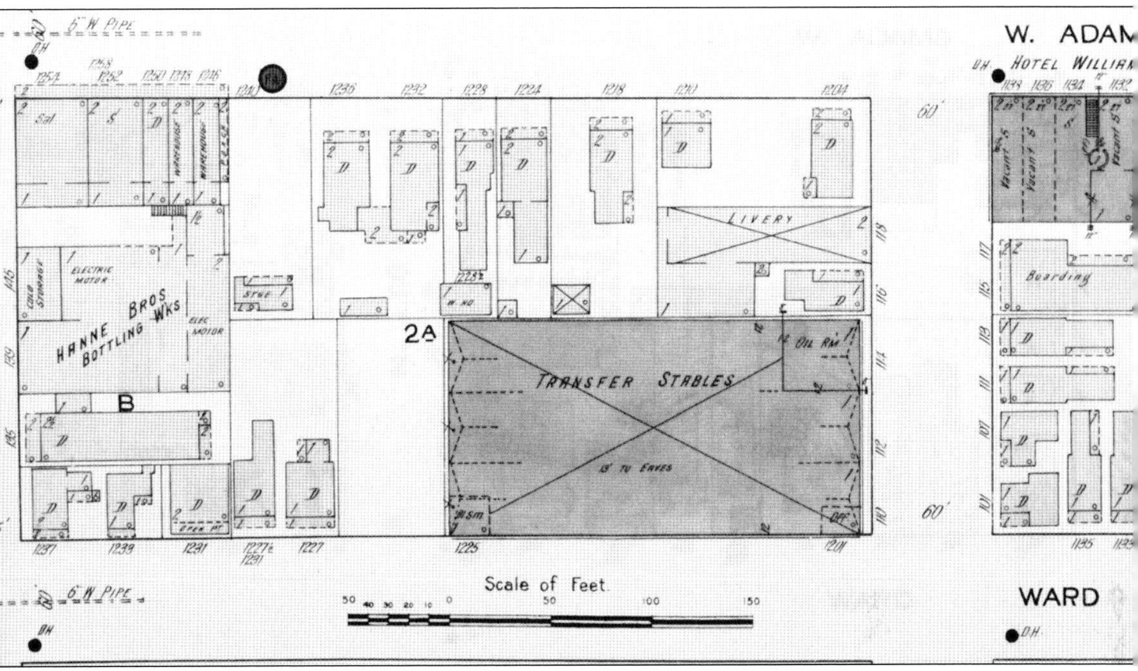

A Sanborn Fire Insurance Company map shows Hanne Bros. Bottling Works on Adams Street. The nearby Ward Street was the previous name of what is now Houston Street. (Courtesy of Library of Congress.)

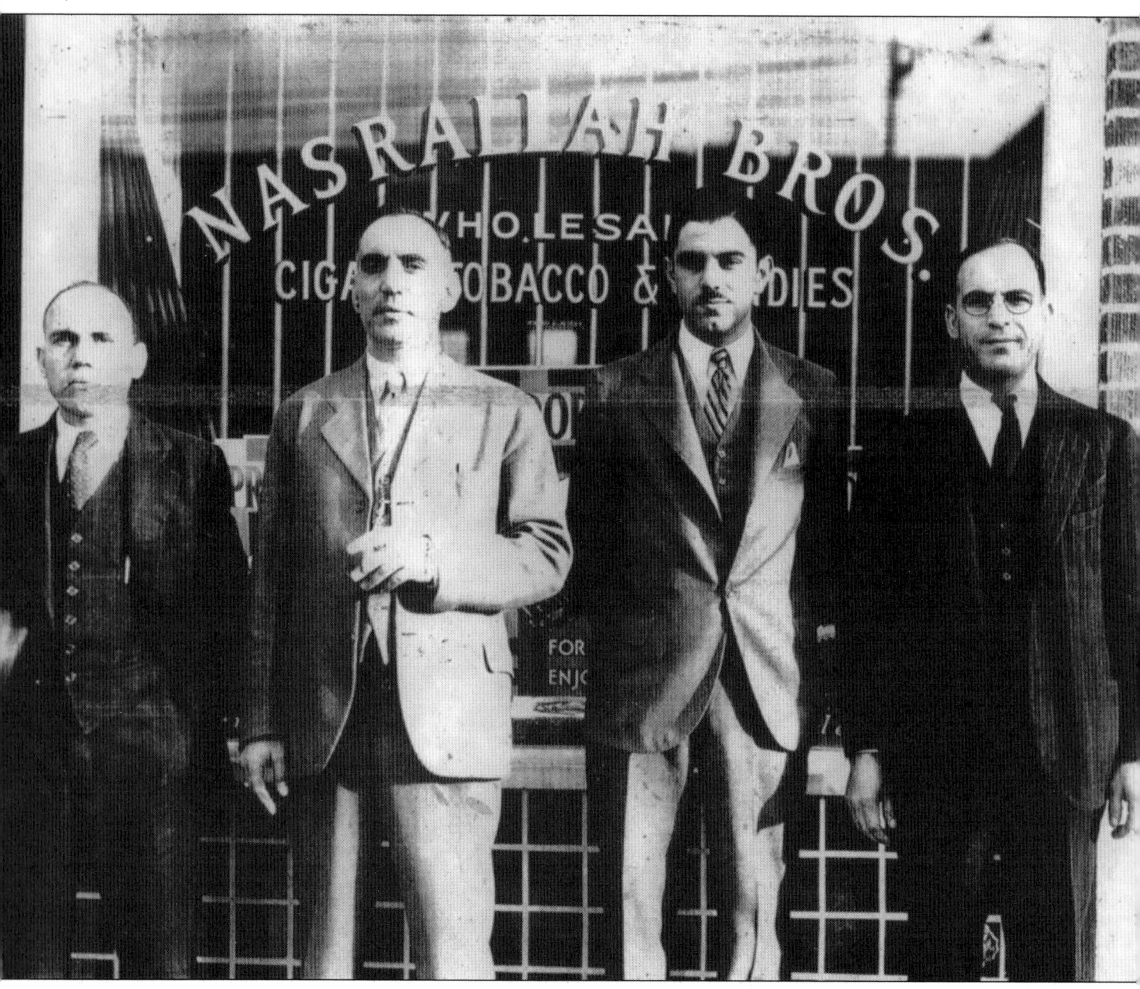

Old Union Beer was brewed in New Orleans by the Union Brewing Company. The Nasrallah brothers sold Old Union beer from their business Union Beer & Wine Company at 914 East Bay Street from 1936 to 1943. The photograph shows the Nasrallah brothers from left to right: A.A. Nasrallah, A.K. Nasrallah, Rudolph Nasrallah, and Nash Nasrallah. (Courtesy of Whiteway Corner Realty.)

Three

JACKSONVILLE'S JAX BEER

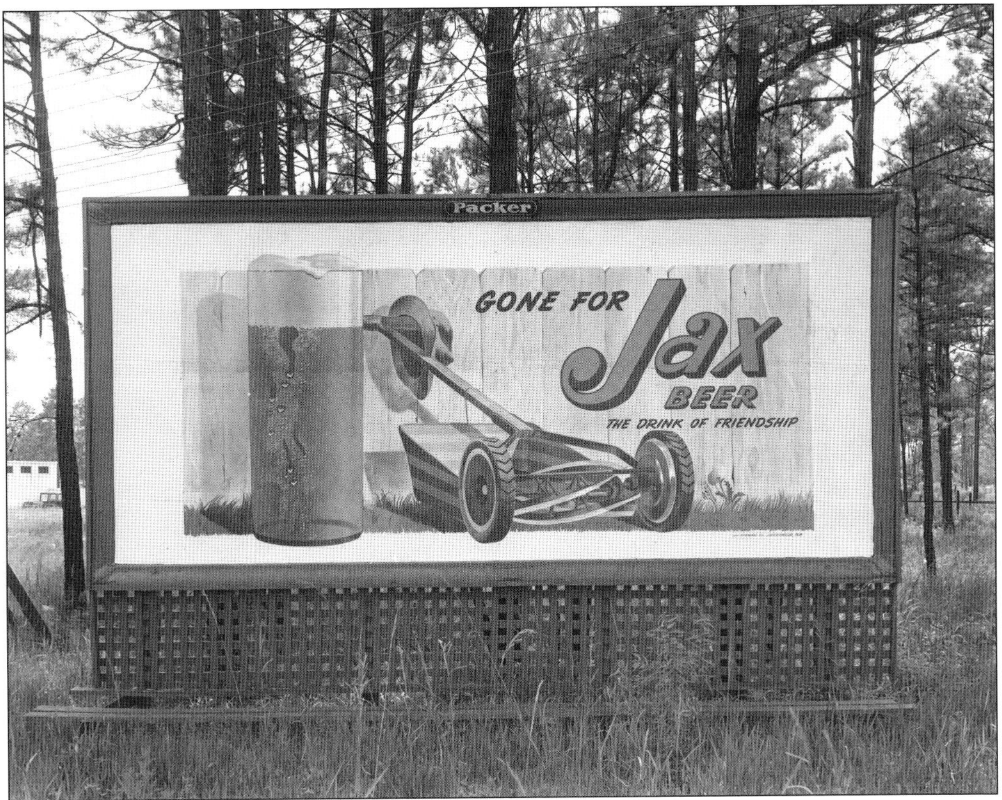

Jax Beer was brewed by the Jacksonville Brewing Company from 1913 to 1918. After Prohibition, from 1933 to 1956, Jax Beer was brewed under the new name Jax Brewing Company. The Jacksonville Brewing Company was Jacksonville's first major local brewery. The photograph shows a billboard advertising Jax Beer in the 1940s. (Courtesy of State Archives of Florida.)

ROYAL PALM AND JAX BEER

Without a Peer in the Country

Brewed From the Choicest Hops and Selected Malt

IN THE NEWEST AND MOST MODERN BREWERY IN AMERICA, UNDER THE DIRECTION OF A SKILLED BREWMASTER.

Royal Palm

AND

Jax Beer

IS BREWED FOR THOSE WHOSE TASTE DEMANDS THE BEST.

BREWED AND BOTTLED UNDER THE MOST SANITARY AND SCIENTIFIC CONDITIONS.

On Sale at all the leading Clubs Cafes and Bars

ORDER A CASE TODAY

OUR "ROYAL PALM" BEER IN CASES READY FOR DELIVERY.

EVERY BOTTLE OF BEER YOU BUY THAT IS MADE IN JACKSONVILLE HELPS YOUR CITY AND STATE—IT KEEPS THE MONEY AT HOME.

YOU ARE CORDIALLY INVITED TO INSPECT OUR BREWERY AND SEE HOW THESE PALATABLE, DELIGHTFUL AND HEALTH-BUILDING BEERS ARE BREWED

If You Have Any Difficulty in Getting Our Beers, Phone 3500

JACKSONVILLE BREWING CO.

Myrtle Ave. and 16th St.   Jacksonville, Florida

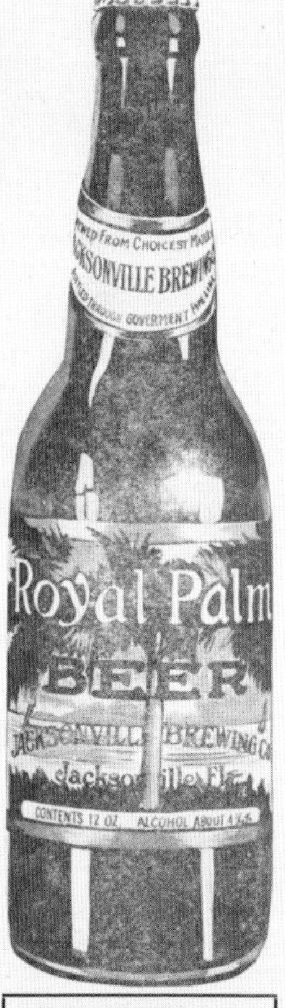

Beers brewed by the Jacksonville Brewing Company included Ostner's Stout, Ostner's Lager Beer, Ostner's Sparkling Ale, Hi Jax Beer, Jax Ale, and Royal Palm Beer. This advertisement shows Royal Palm along with the Jax Beer brand in 1914. Royal Palm Beer was a Bohemian-style pilsner. (Courtesy of Jacksonville Public Library.)

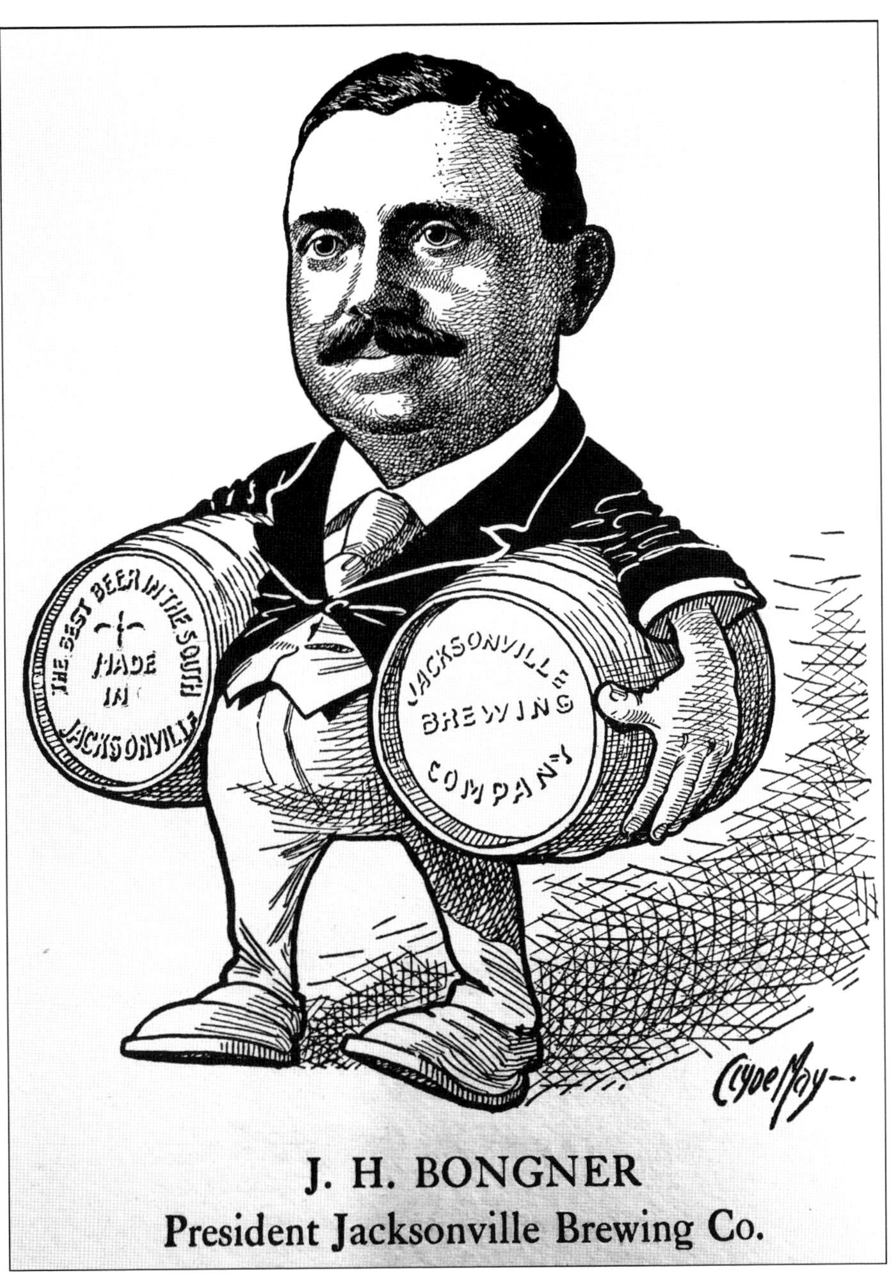

J. H. BONGNER
President Jacksonville Brewing Co.

Jacob Bongner was the president of the Jacksonville Brewing Company. When Prohibition was enacted, he was surprised it would happen and that the American public would ever enact laws prohibiting the brewing of beer. Bongner was forced to let go of 243 employees of the Jacksonville Brewing Company because of Prohibition. With a previous investment of $300,000 of his own money into the Jacksonville Brewing Company, Bongner then had to decide how to adapt the Jacksonville Brewing Company during Prohibition. The Jacksonville Brewing Company under Bongner was rebranded, renamed the Jax Ice and Cold Storage Company, and converted into a cold storage facility. From 1919 to 1924, the company under Bongner diversified to stay in business during Prohibition by producing ice cream, near beer, ginger ale, and ice. In 1924, Bongner passed away, leading to William Ostner becoming president of the Jax Ice and Cold Storage Company. (Courtesy of Jacksonville Public Library.)

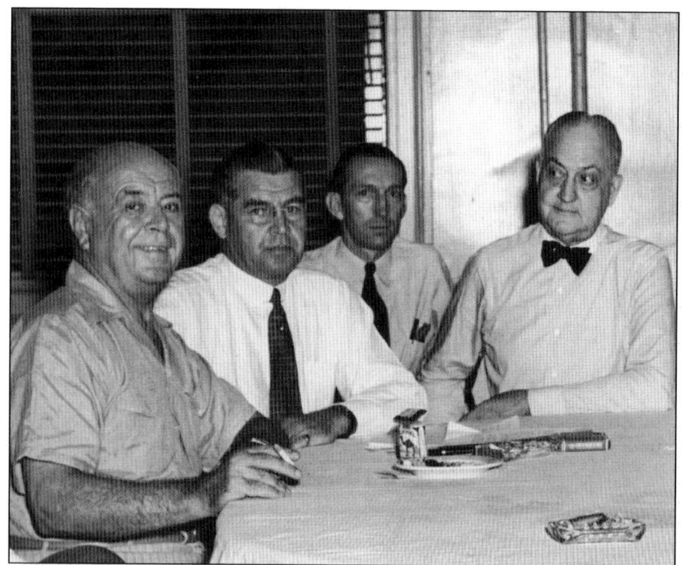

William Ostner was born Wilhelm Ostner on May 9, 1877, in Baden, Germany. Ostner moved to St. Louis, where he became a master brewer at Otto Stifel's Union Brewery. Ostner relocated to Jacksonville in 1913 and applied his knowledge of brewing with the creation of the Jacksonville Brewing Company. The photograph shows Ostner holding a cigarette with Jax Brewing Company employees in the 1940s. (Courtesy of Jacksonville Historical Society.)

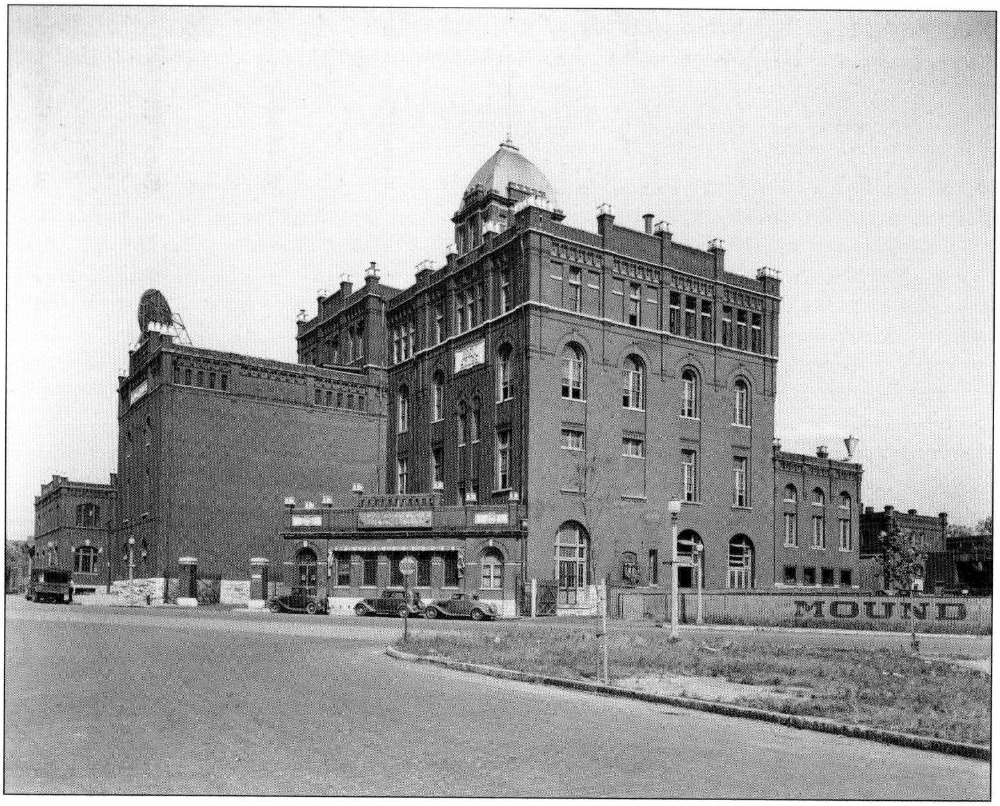

Jacob Schorr and Henry Kolkschneider founded the Schorr-Kolkschneider Brewing Company in 1902 in St. Louis. Jacob's daughter Caroline Schorr married William Ostner in 1911. Ostner's father-in-law, Jacob Schorr, helped him establish the Jacksonville Brewing Company, with the first brew released in 1914. Ostner's brother-in-law John Schorr was an initial stockholder in the Jacksonville Brewing Company. The photograph shows the Schorr-Kolkschneider Brewing Company in St. Louis in 1935. (Courtesy of Missouri Historical Society.)

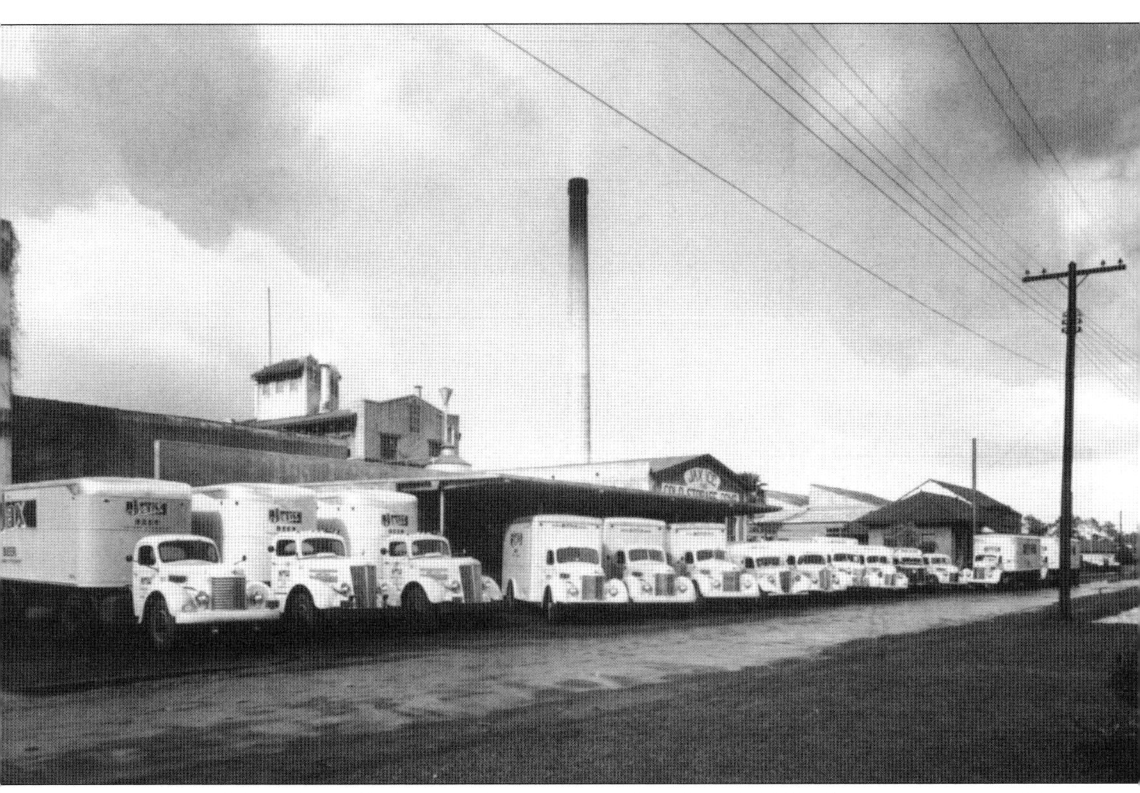

Construction of the Jacksonville Brewing Company started on June 9, 1913. The initial capacity of the brewing plant was 30,000 barrels of beer per year. It was the second brewery built in Florida after the Florida Brewing Company and the last brewery built before Prohibition. During Prohibition, the brewery was renamed the Jacksonville Ice and Cold Storage Company, which provided cold storage to businesses and manufactured ice cream. The brewery produced nonalcoholic beverages called "near beer," which had less than 0.5 percent alcohol by volume. After Prohibition, the Jacksonville Ice and Cold Storage Company restarted production of its Jax Beer brand under the Jax Brewing Company name. This photograph from the 1940s shows the name "Jax Ice and Cold Storage Company" on the Jax Brewing Company building in the center. (Courtesy of Jacksonville Historical Society.)

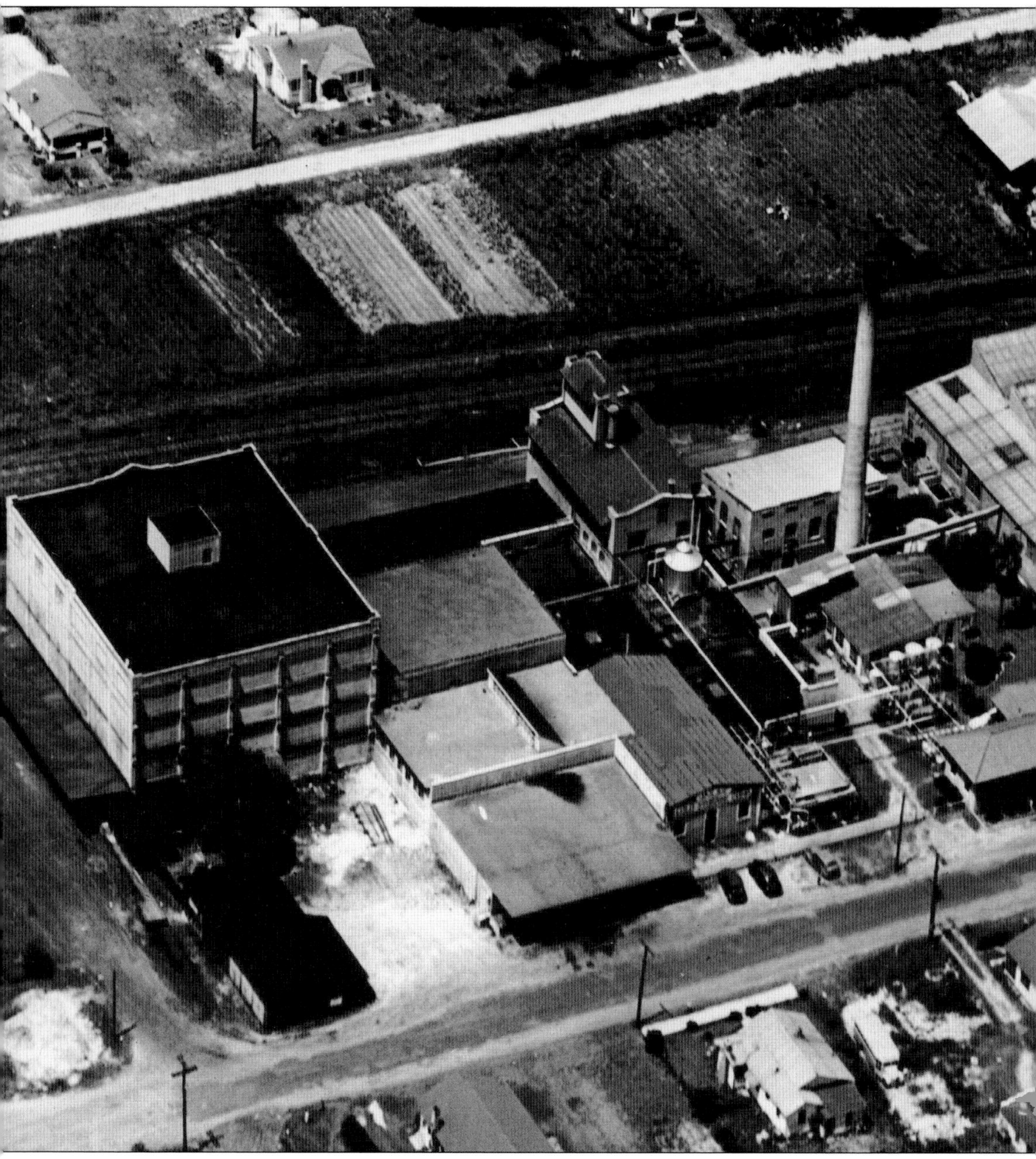

In 1918, the Jacksonville Brewing Company was renamed the Jax Ice and Cold Storage Company. In May 1919, an ice cream plant was completed. In 1921, an ice plant was added to its brewery. A four-story cold storage facility opened in 1925 to keep up with demand. The aerial photograph from the 1940s shows the

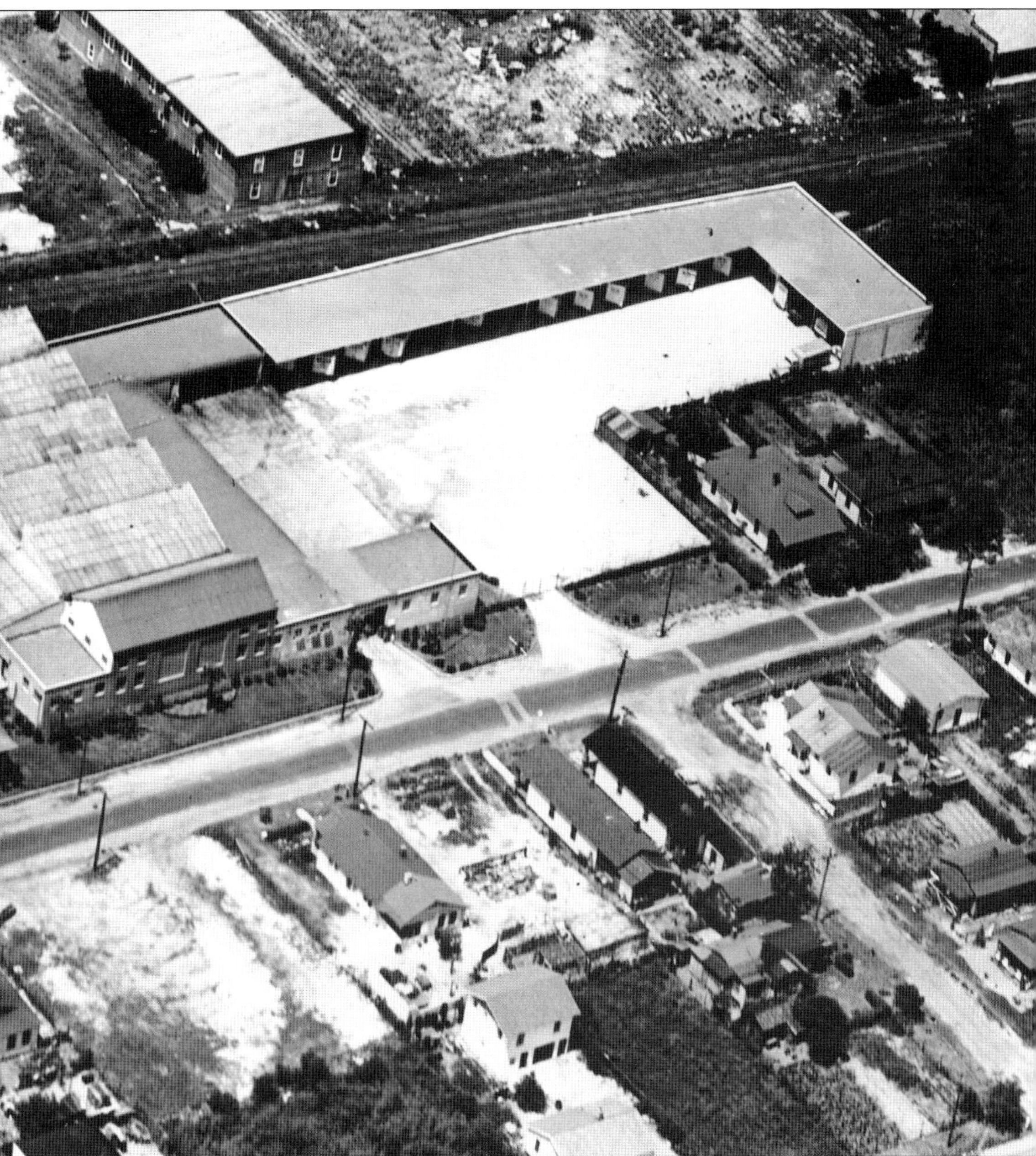

Jax Ice and Cold Storage Company property on West Sixteenth Street. The brewhouse can be seen in the center left next to the smokestack. The backs of delivery trucks can be seen at the shipping dock on the right. (Courtesy of Jacksonville Historical Society.)

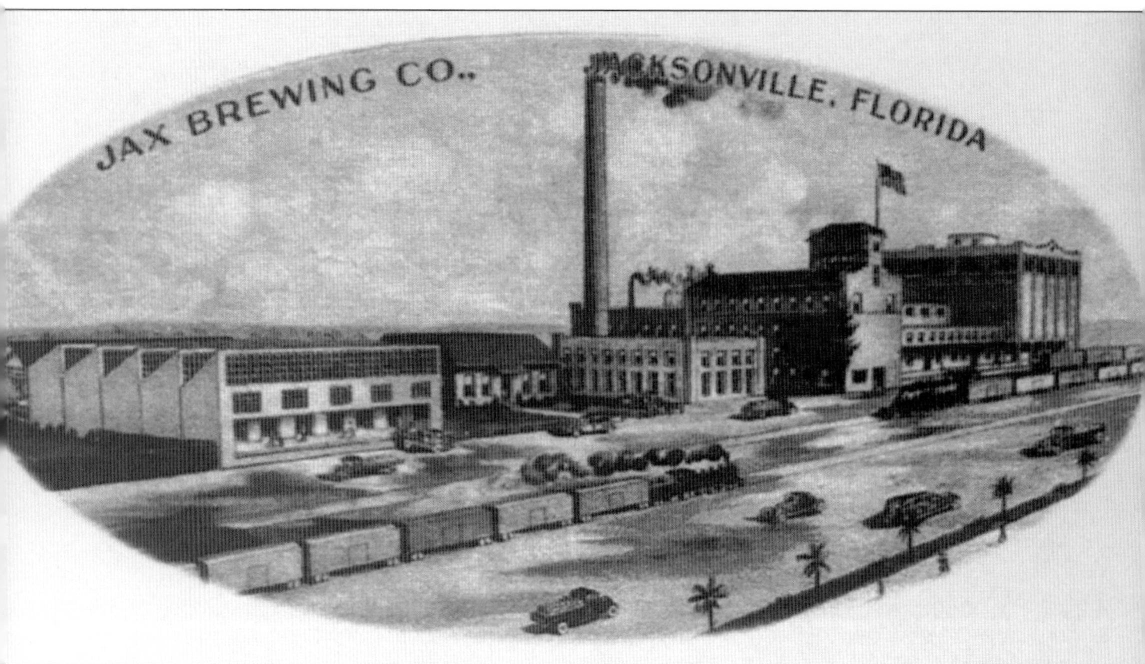

When the brewery restarted after Prohibition, it was renamed the Jax Brewing Company. The Jax Ice and Cold Storage Company continued its cold storage business while operating the brewery. This logo of the Jax Brewing Company from a letterhead dates to the 1940s. (Jacksonville Historical Preservation Commission.)

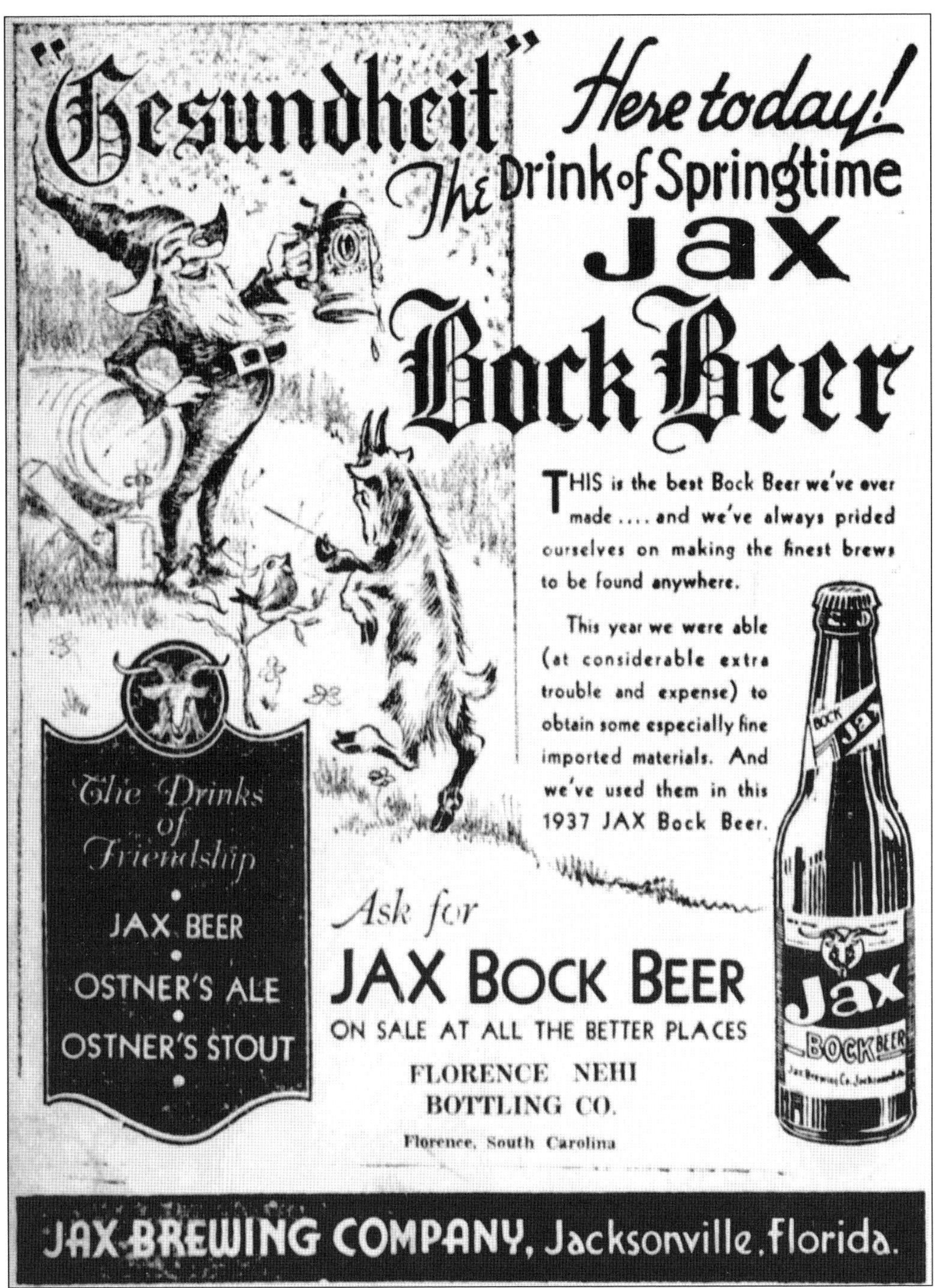

This 1937 advertisement from the *Columbia Record* shows Jax Brewing Company's own bock beer. Bock beer is a traditional German dark lager with a higher alcohol content. Also in the advertisement are Jax Beer, Ostner's Ale, and Ostner's Stout. (Courtesy of *Columbia Record*.)

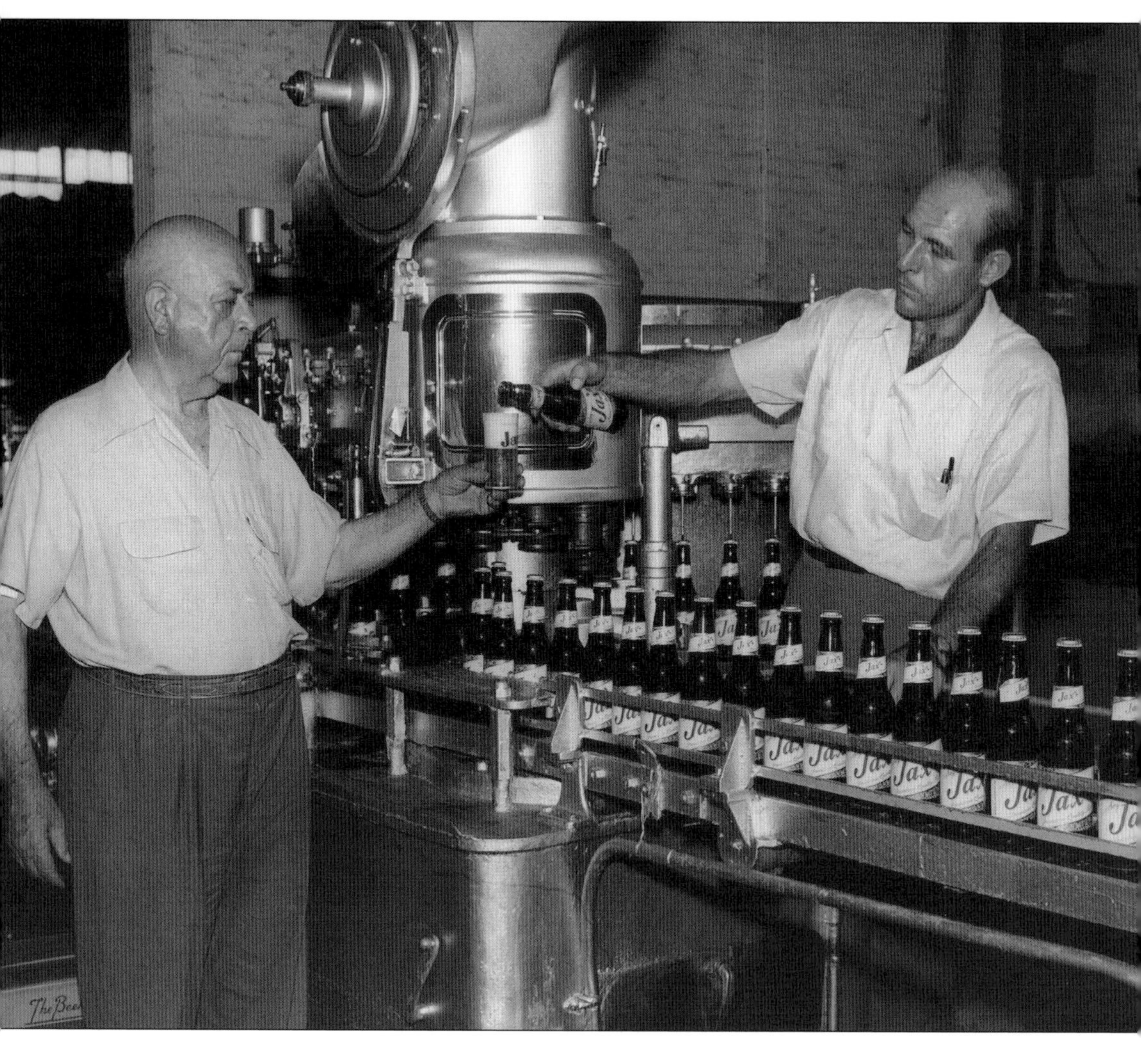

Several breweries and businesses lay claim to inventing the concept of the six-pack, including the Jax Brewing Company. In the 1940s, Jax Beer was sold six to a sack at $1.29. The photograph shows William Ostner and his son William Albert "Bill" Ostner at the Jax Brewing Company facility in the 1950s. (Courtesy of Loyd Sandgren.)

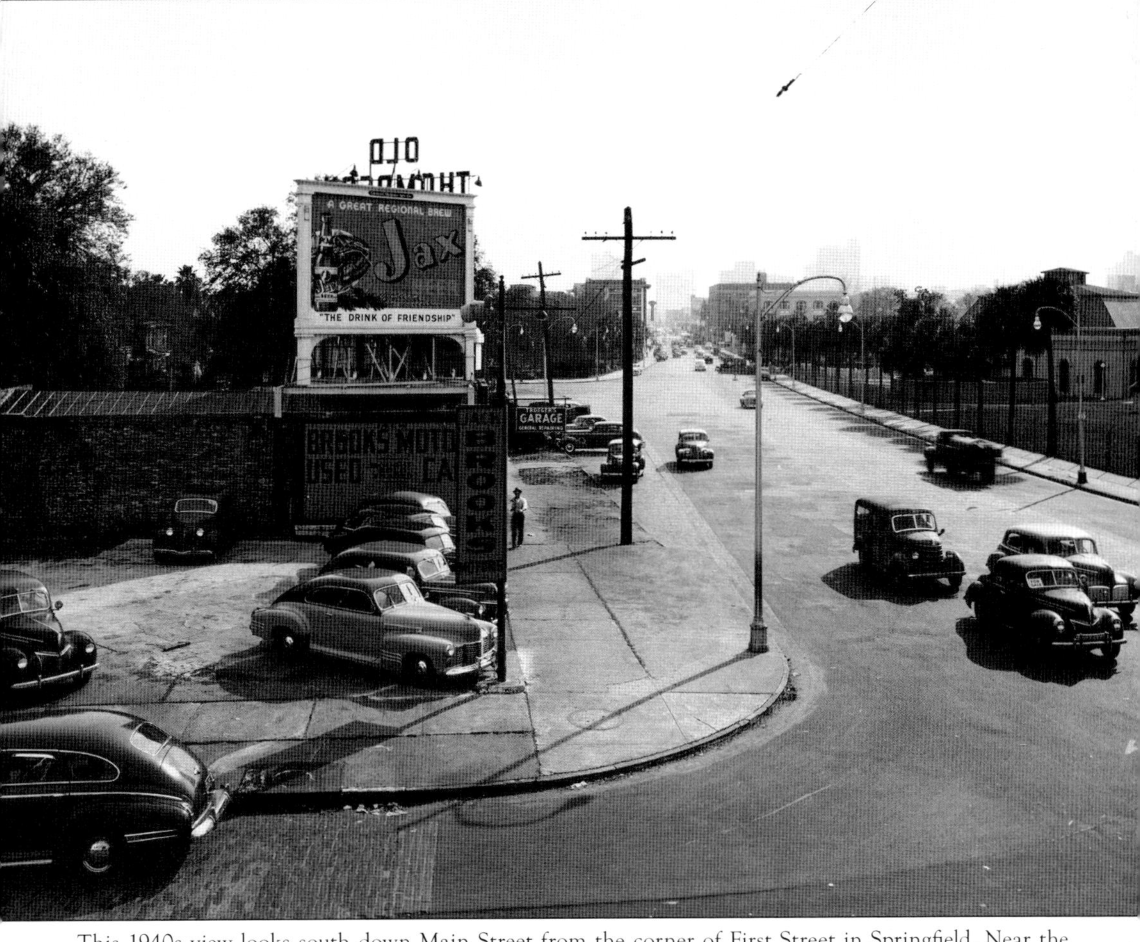

This 1940s view looks south down Main Street from the corner of First Street in Springfield. Near the center of the photograph is a Jax Beer billboard over the roof of Jack Brooks Motors and Troger's Garage. According to William Ostner, who was president of the Florida Brewers Association, Florida was the largest beer-producing state south of Baltimore and east of New Orleans in 1944 with a total production of 484,377 barrels of beer produced. (Courtesy of Loyd Sandgren.)

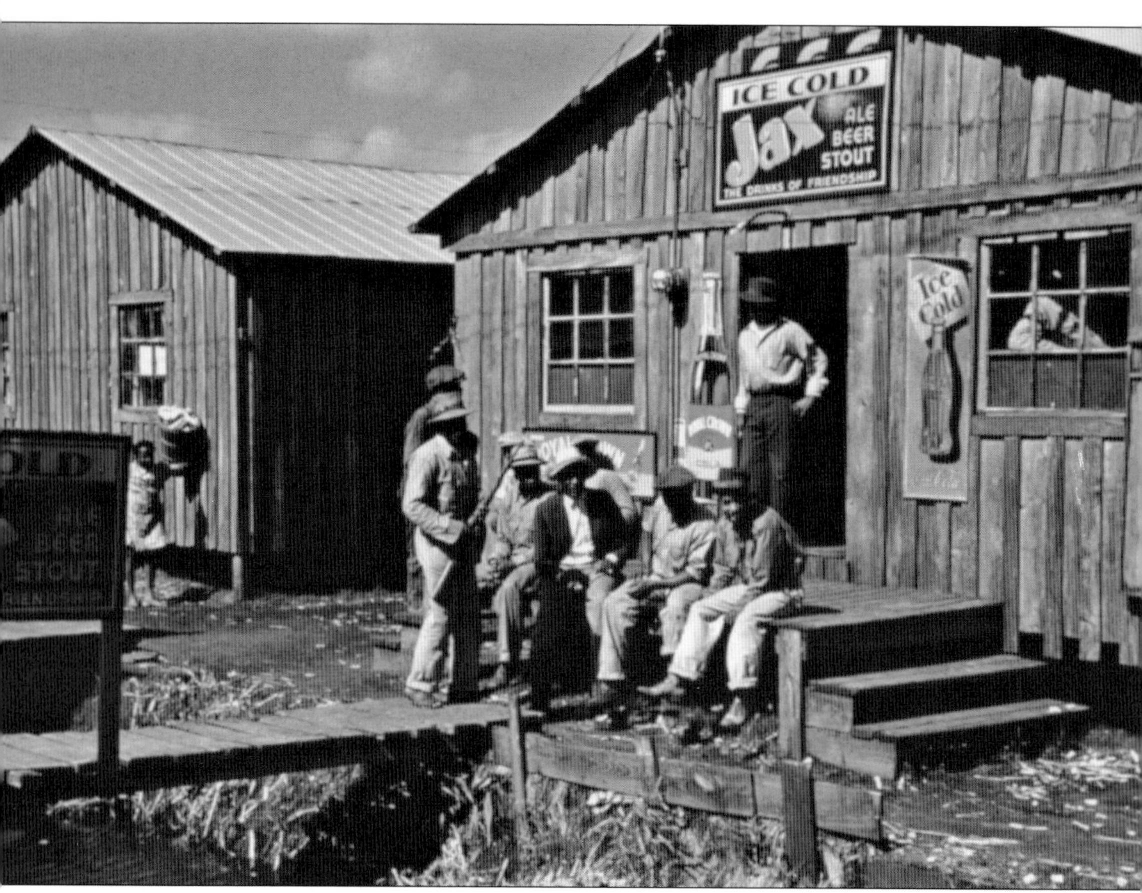

Jax Beer was distributed throughout Florida and the southeastern United States. This photograph depicts living quarters for migratory workers in Belle Glade in 1944. A sign for Jax Beer can be seen on the building and in front of the workers. Belle Glade is located near Lake Okeechobee in South Florida. In 1935, a legal dispute arose over the Jax Beer name between the Jax Brewing Company and the Jackson Brewing Company of New Orleans. Founded in 1890, the Jackson Brewing Company brewed a beer also called Jax Beer. A compromise was reached where the Jax Brewing Company would distribute its Jax Beer in Florida, Georgia, and the Carolinas. The Jackson Brewing Company in turn would distribute its Jax Beer in the western states. (Courtesy of Library of Congress.)

The photograph shows a woman drinking a Jax
Beer from the Jackson Brewing Company at a
crab boil in Raceland, Louisiana, in 1938. The
Jackson Brewing Company used a silhouette
of Andrew Jackson on a horse as part of its
logo. The Jax Brewing Company Jax Beer
logo had a cockatoo with the phrase "Say Jax"
next to it above the words "Jax Pilsner Style
Beer." (Courtesy of Library of Congress.)

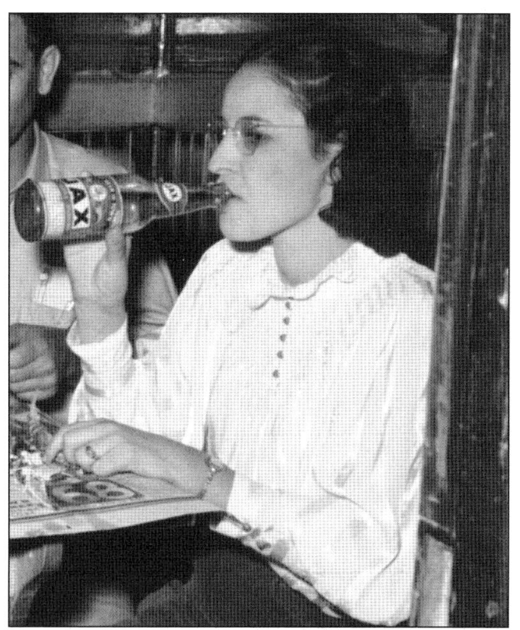

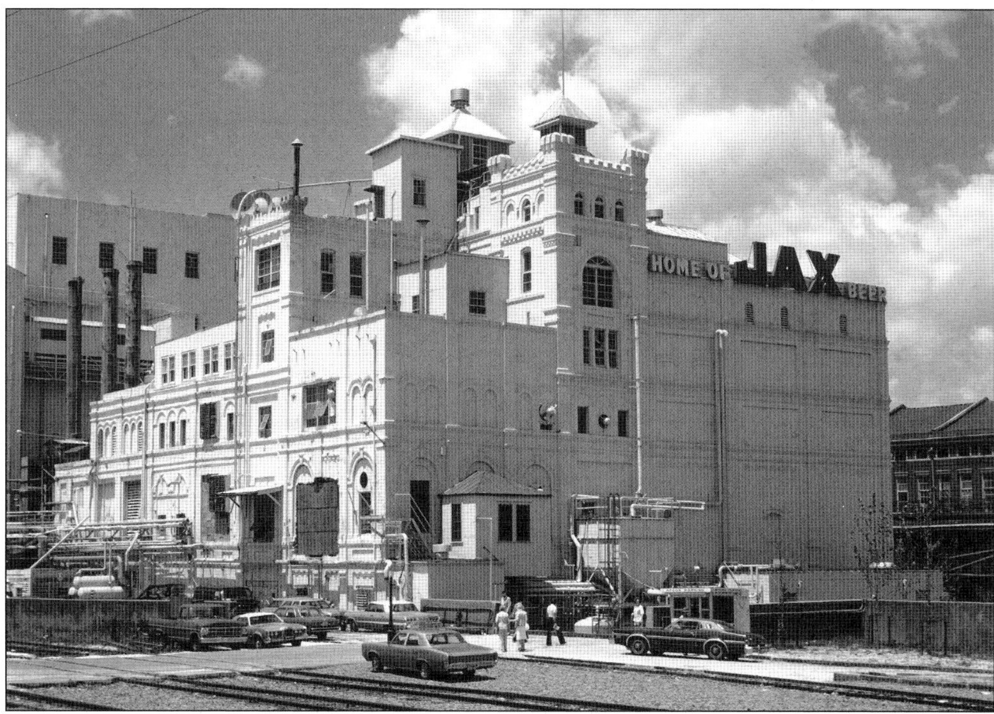

In 1956, the Jax Ice and Cold Storage Company shut down its brewery, effectively ending the Jax Brewing
Company. The Jax Brewing Company sold its copyright of the Jax Beer brand to the New Orleans–based
Jackson Brewing Company, which then enabled it to distribute its own Jax Beer brand throughout the
southeastern United States. The photograph from 1976 shows the famous Jackson Brewery Company
building in New Orleans with its trademark sign "Home of Jax Beer." The Jackson Brewery Company
building is still standing in New Orleans and has been converted into a commercial space for stores and
restaurants. (Courtesy of Leon Winer.)

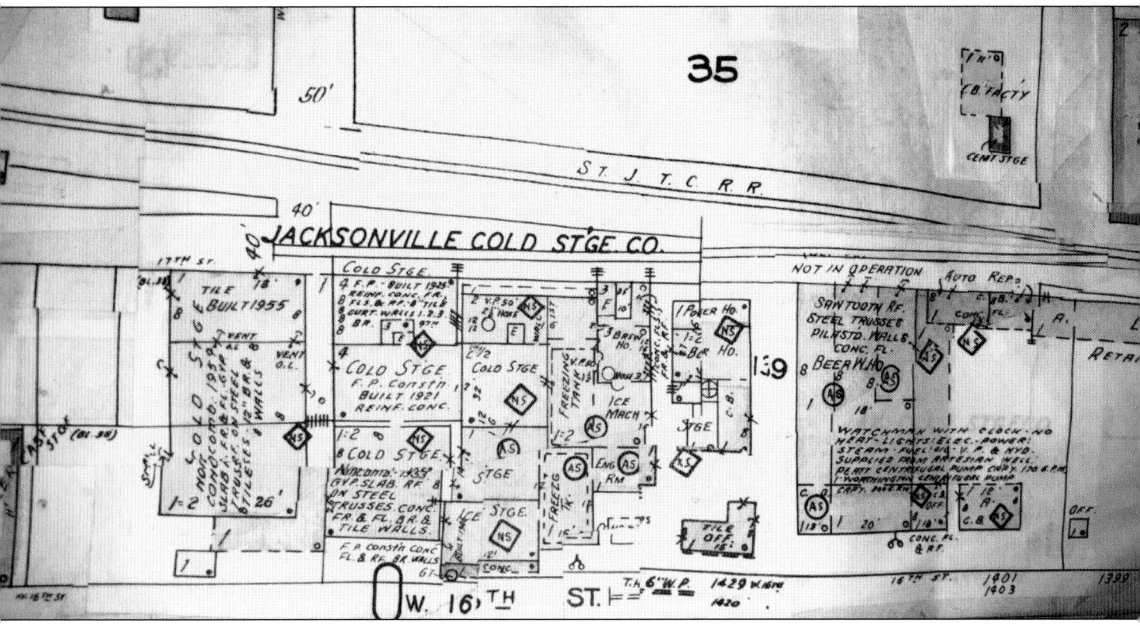

The Jax Ice and Cold Storage Company under William Ostner's son William A. Ostner returned to its Prohibition-era state after 1956 by discontinuing brewing operations permanently. Brewing Jax Beer in the 1950s had no longer made a profit for the Jax Ice and Cold Storage Company because of the change in demand and growth of overall better beer from out of state. With no more use for the brewing equipment, it was sold and salvaged for $60,000. (Courtesy of Library of Congress.)

Four

ANHEUSER-BUSCH AND JACKSONVILLE

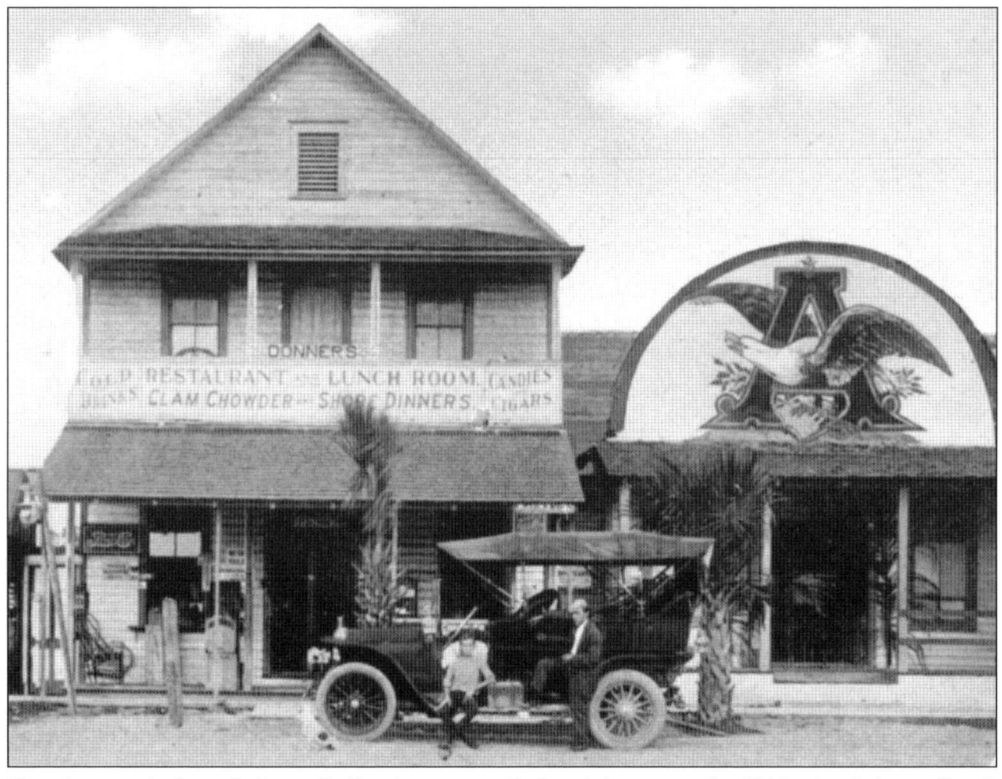

The photograph shows Jacksonville Beach stores on Railroad Avenue in the 1900s. An Anheuser-Busch sign can be seen on top of the store on the right. The letter A in the logo stands for Anheuser. (Courtesy of Library of Congress.)

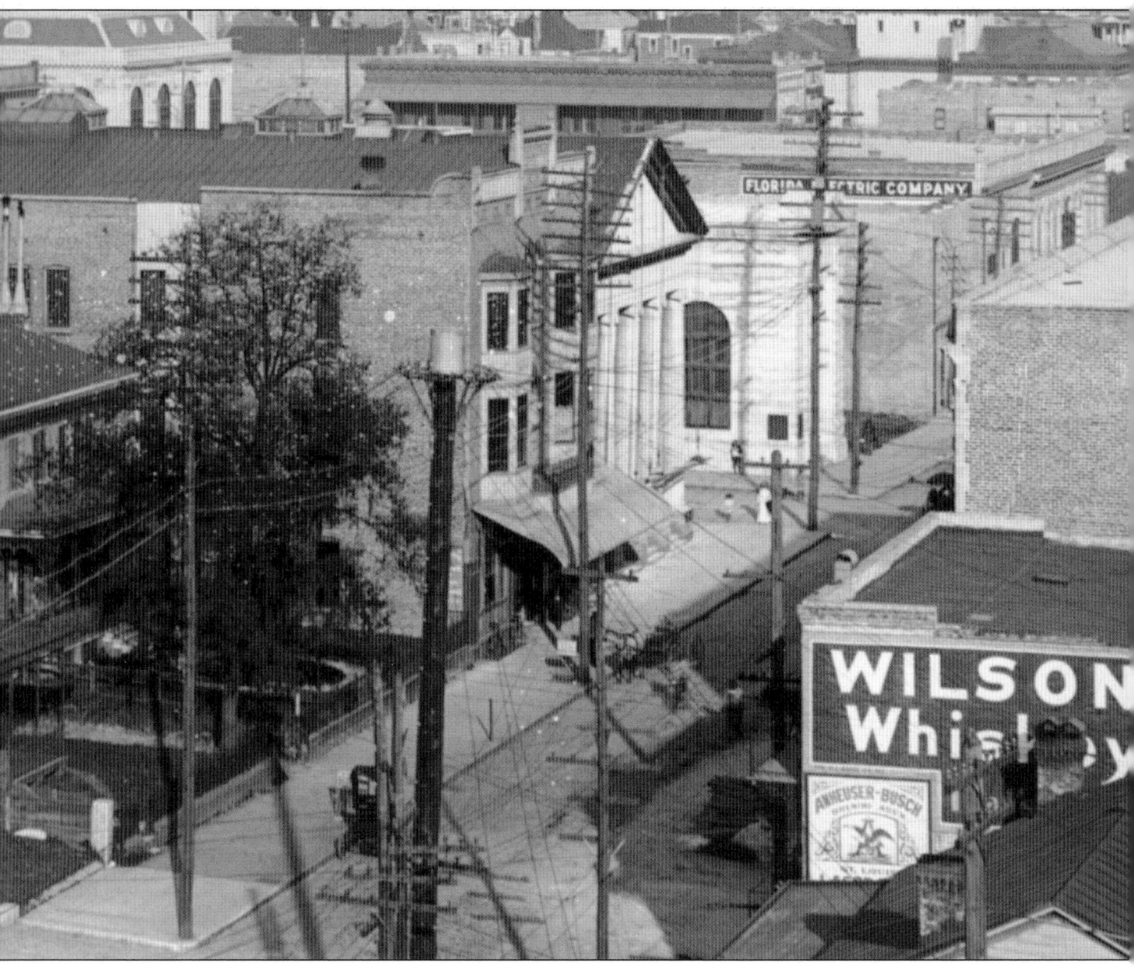

By 1907, Anheuser-Busch was producing around 1.6 million barrels of beer in St. Louis, becoming a well-recognized name in the brewing industry. Anheuser-Busch first made an appearance in Jacksonville in the 1890s through its distributor, the Jos. Zapf Company. The photograph shows Adams Street in Jacksonville around 1904. In the lower right is a building that says "Wilson Whiskey" with an advertisement for Anheuser-Busch underneath. (Courtesy of Library of Congress.)

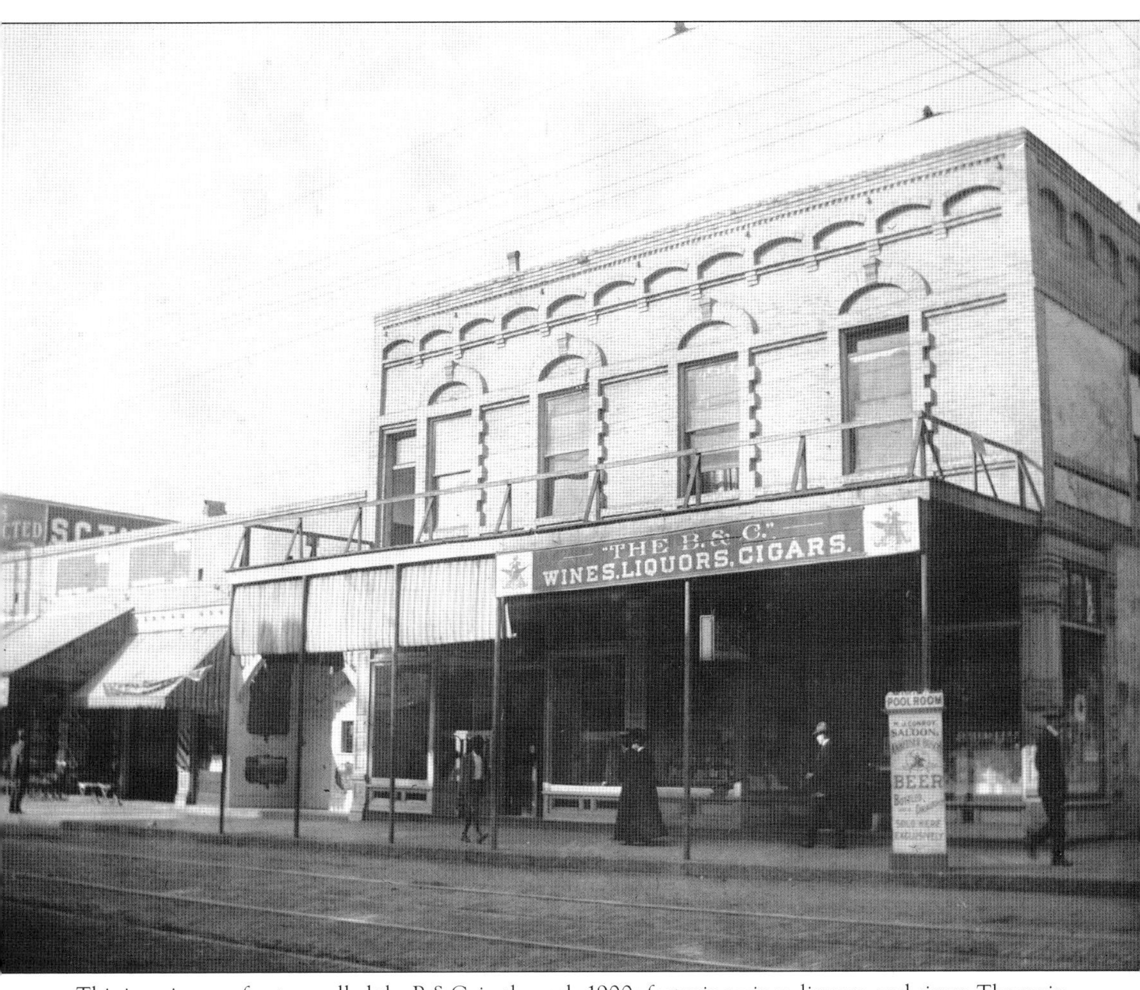

This is an image of a store called the B.&C. in the early 1900s featuring wines, liquors, and cigars. The main beer promoted by the store is Anheuser-Busch. (Courtesy of Jacksonville Historical Society.)

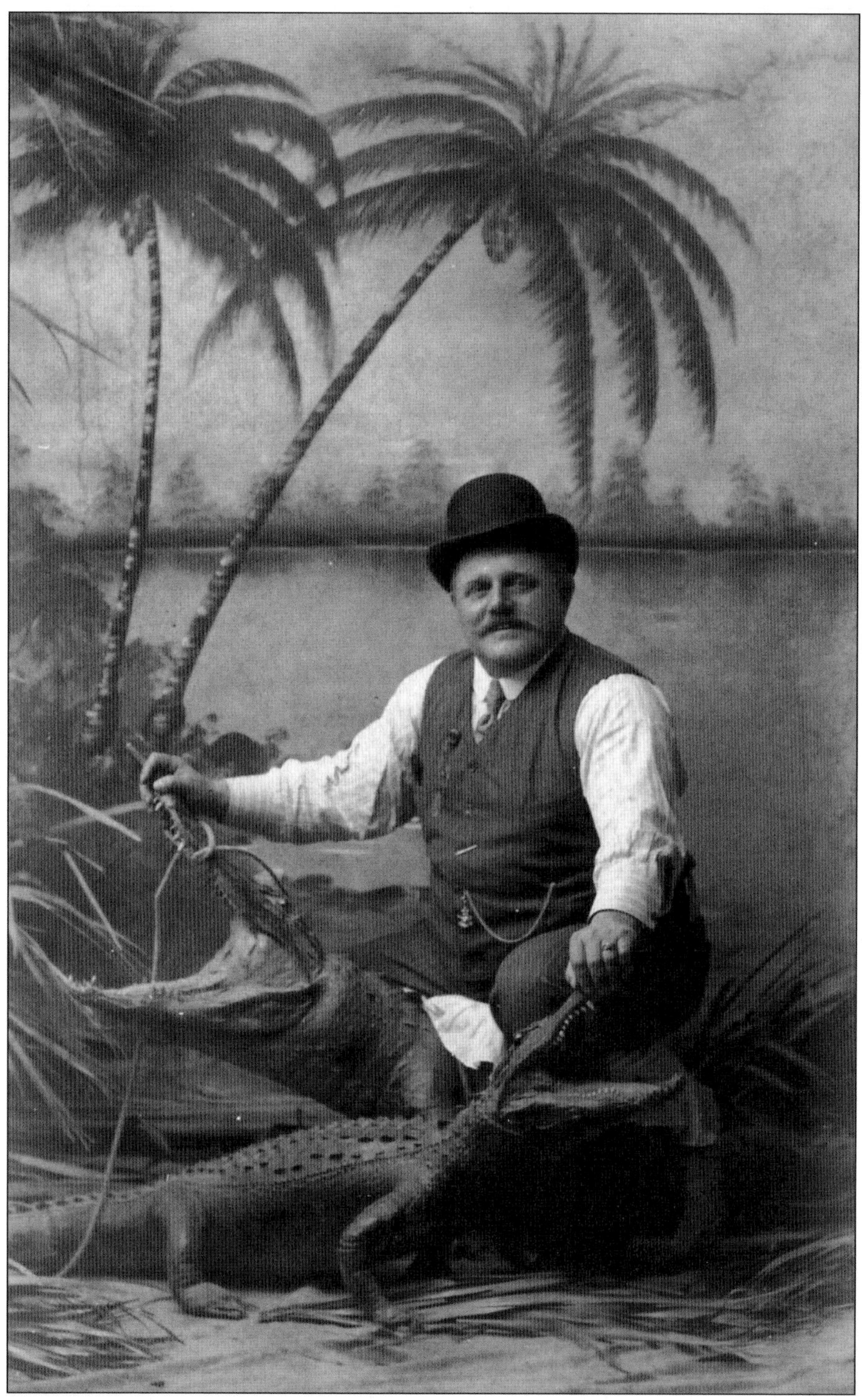

Franz Joseph Zapf was born on August 19, 1860, in Germany. In the early 1880s, Zapf immigrated to Joplin, Missouri, where at some point he decided to drop Franz and be called Joseph Zapf. In 1887, Zapf married Mary Danner Muller. That same year, he moved to Jacksonville, where he would pursue his Anheuser-Busch distribution business, Jos. Zapf & Co. (Courtesy of National Archives.)

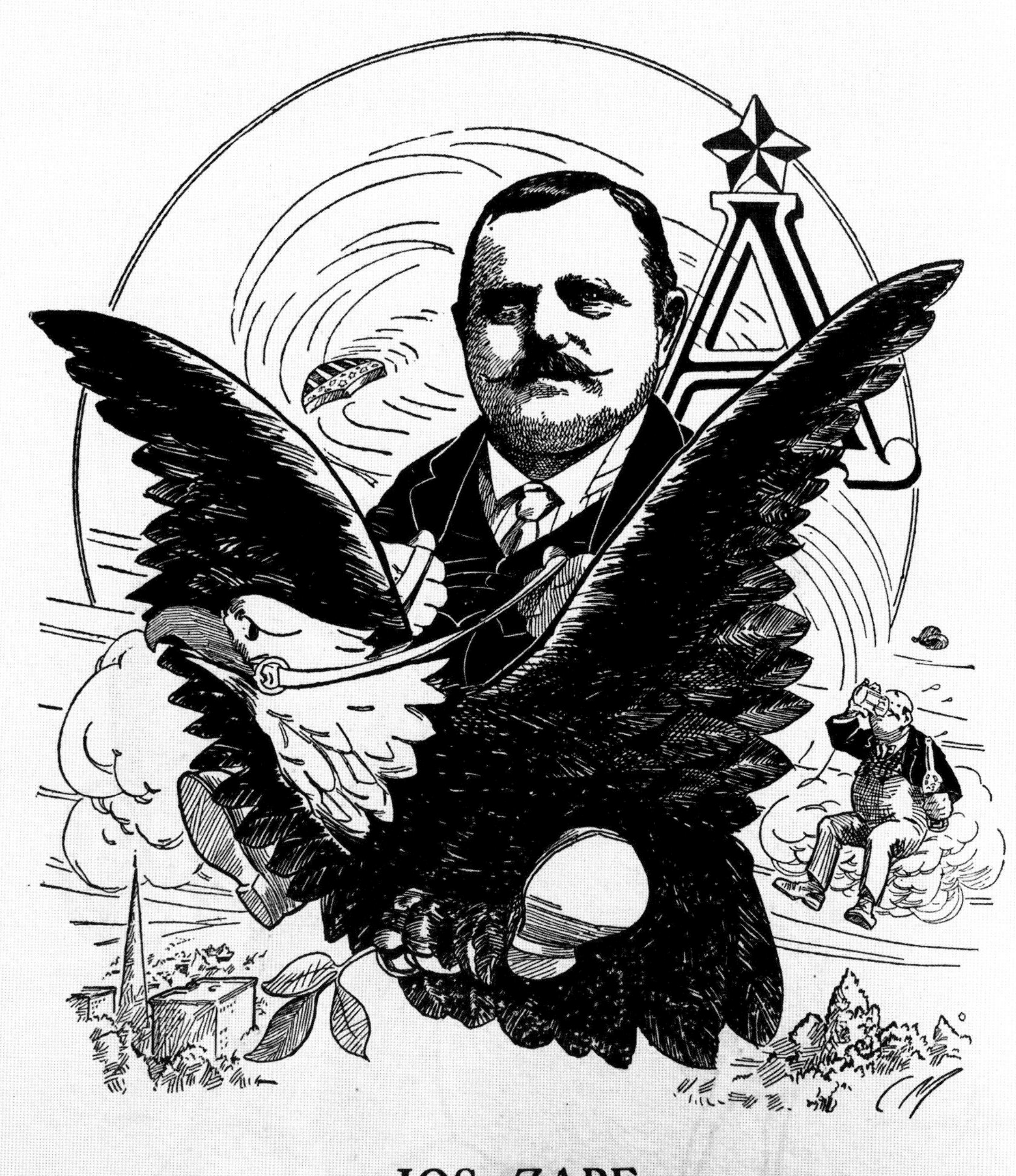

In the 1890s, the Jos. Zapf Company became the distributor of Anheuser-Busch beer in North Florida. Anheuser-Busch brewing was done at its St. Louis plant until its second brewery was built in Newark, New Jersey, which opened in 1951. Zapf received barrels from Anheuser-Busch in St. Louis and then decanted into bottles. The sketch shows Joseph Zapf and the Anheuser-Busch A. (Courtesy of Jacksonville Public Library.)

This advertisement for Joseph Zapf & Co. is from 1906. Zapf not only bottled Anheuser-Busch but also whiskeys, wines, and mineral waters. Zapf was also an agent for Henry George Cigars, which were notable for being only 5¢. (Courtesy of *Jacksonville Sun*.)

During Prohibition, Anheuser-Busch managed to stay in business by manufacturing corn syrup, near beer, and ginger ale. The Joseph Zapf Company rebranded as Atlantic Distributing Company while still being an agent for Anheuser-Busch. Atlantic Distributing Company distributed Anheuser-Busch's ginger ale during Prohibition. (Courtesy of University of North Florida.)

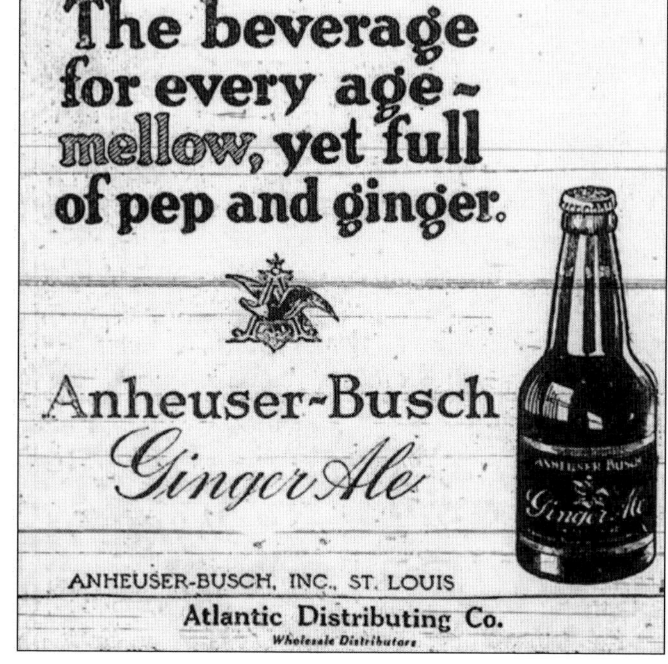

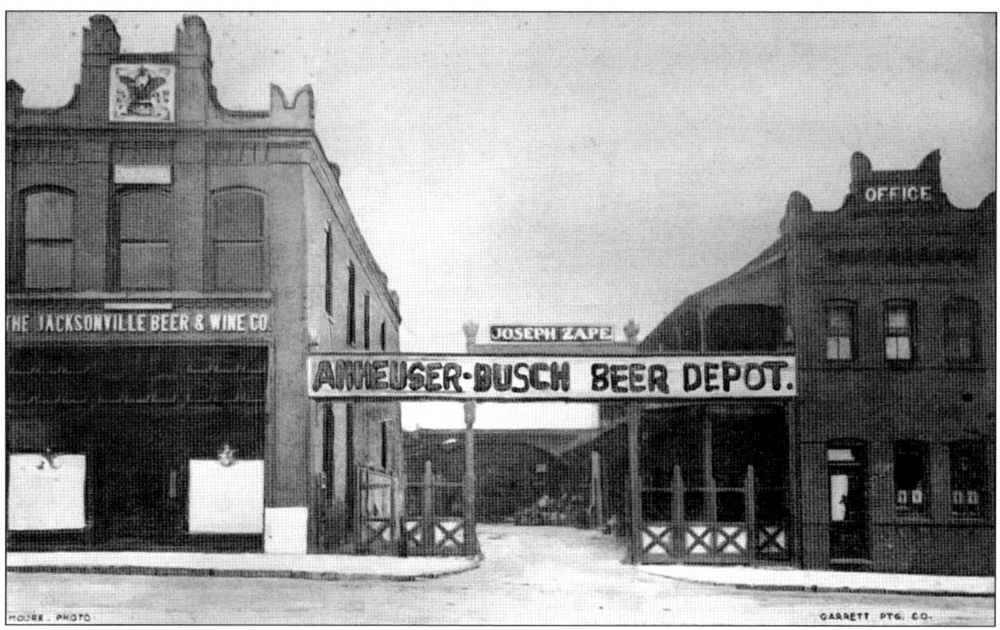

The Anheuser-Busch beer depot of the Jos. Zapf Company on Bay Street is pictured in the early 1900s. The Jacksonville Beer & Wine Company, to the left of the depot, was acquired by Zapf in 1898 and was located at 112 West Bay Street. Zapf also operated a saloon in connection with his Anheuser-Busch Bay Street property. This area is now occupied by the CSX building. Anheuser-Busch has been distributed in the Jacksonville area by North Florida Sales since 1995. (Courtesy of Jacksonville Historical Society.)

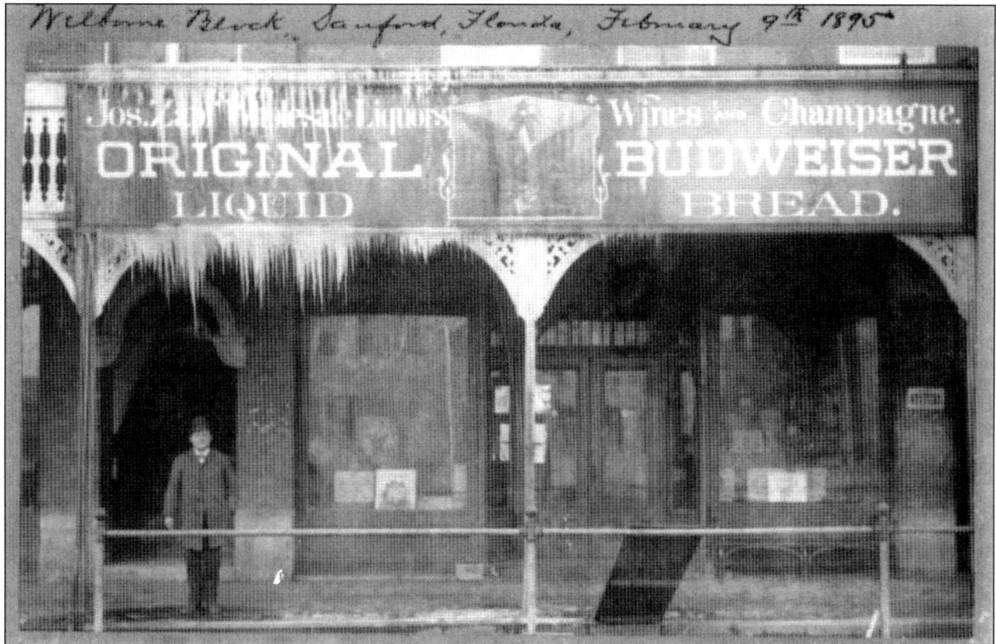

Before Zapf came to Jacksonville, he was a leading merchant in Sanford. Zapf had a store where he sold liquor, wine, and beer. The photograph shows Zapf standing under his store sign with icicles above him in Sanford. The photograph was taken during the Great Freeze, when temperatures as far down as West Palm Beach reached 27 degrees Fahrenheit. (Courtesy of Museum of Seminole County History.)

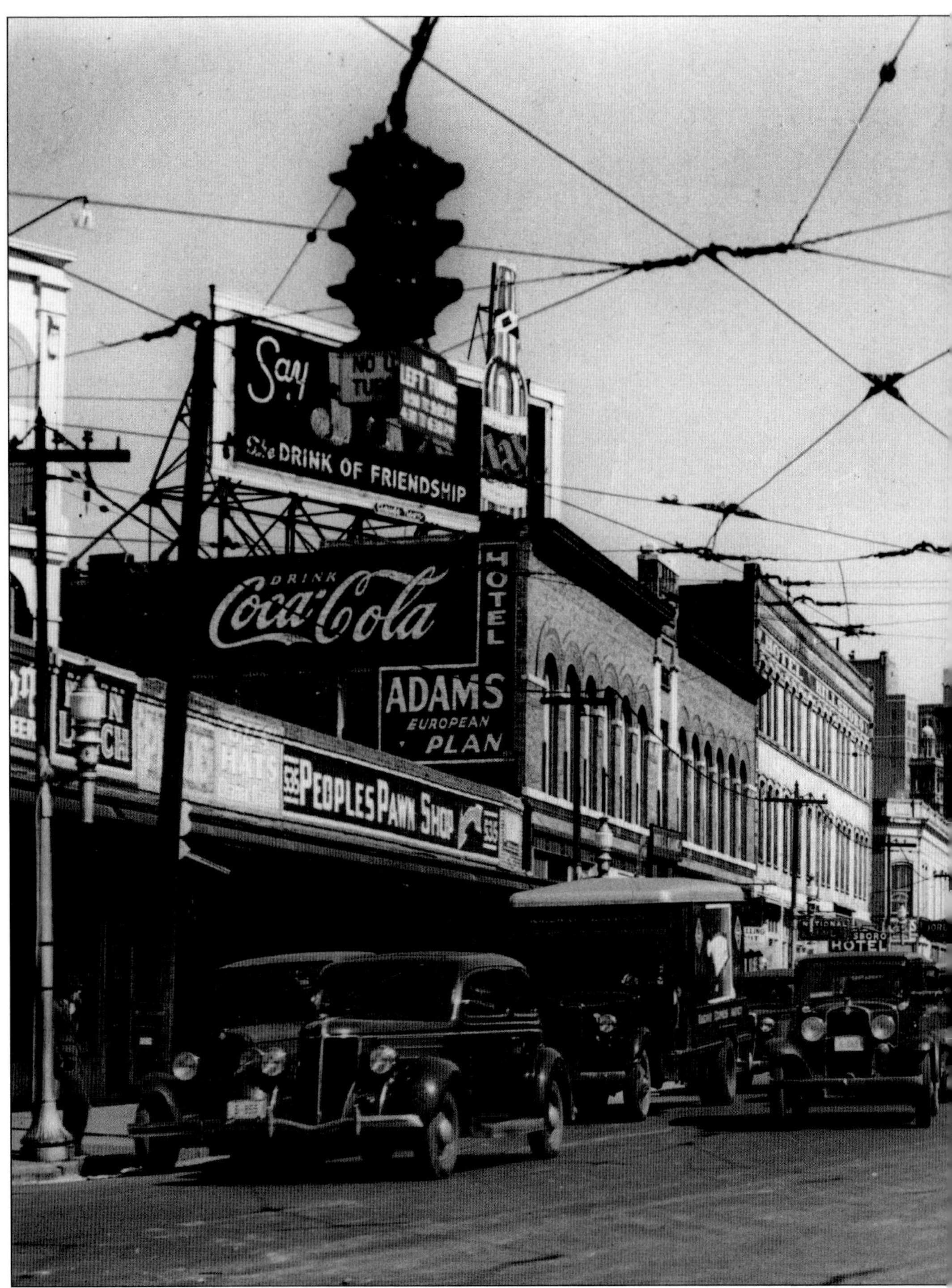

The origin of Budweiser goes back to the former Kingdom of Bohemia, where a German town called Budweis, now called České Budějovice and in the Czech Republic, was brewing beer dating back to the 13th century. The term "Budweiser Bier" was in use by the 16th century, which means beer from Budweis. Adolphus Busch encountered Budweiser beer throughout Europe on his overseas trips. Busch decided to

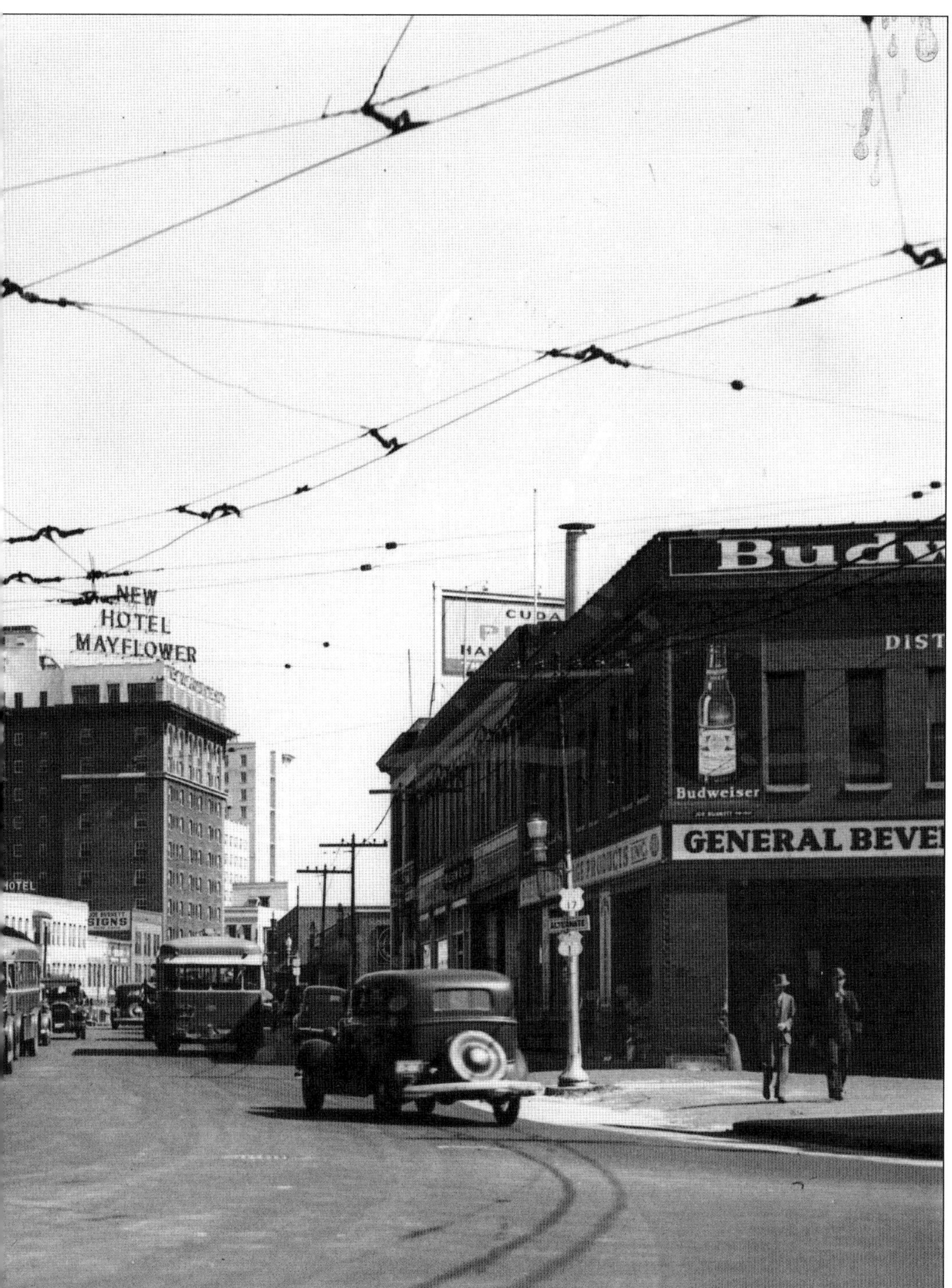

create a new beer based on the Bohemian style of Budweiser. Anheuser-Busch's Budweiser was introduced in 1876, becoming one of its most popular beer brands. The photograph from the 1930s shows a Budweiser bottle and the letters "Budweiser" on a building to the far right on Forsyth Street. Toward the far-left corner is a billboard for Jax Beer behind the traffic light. (Courtesy of Jacksonville Historical Society.)

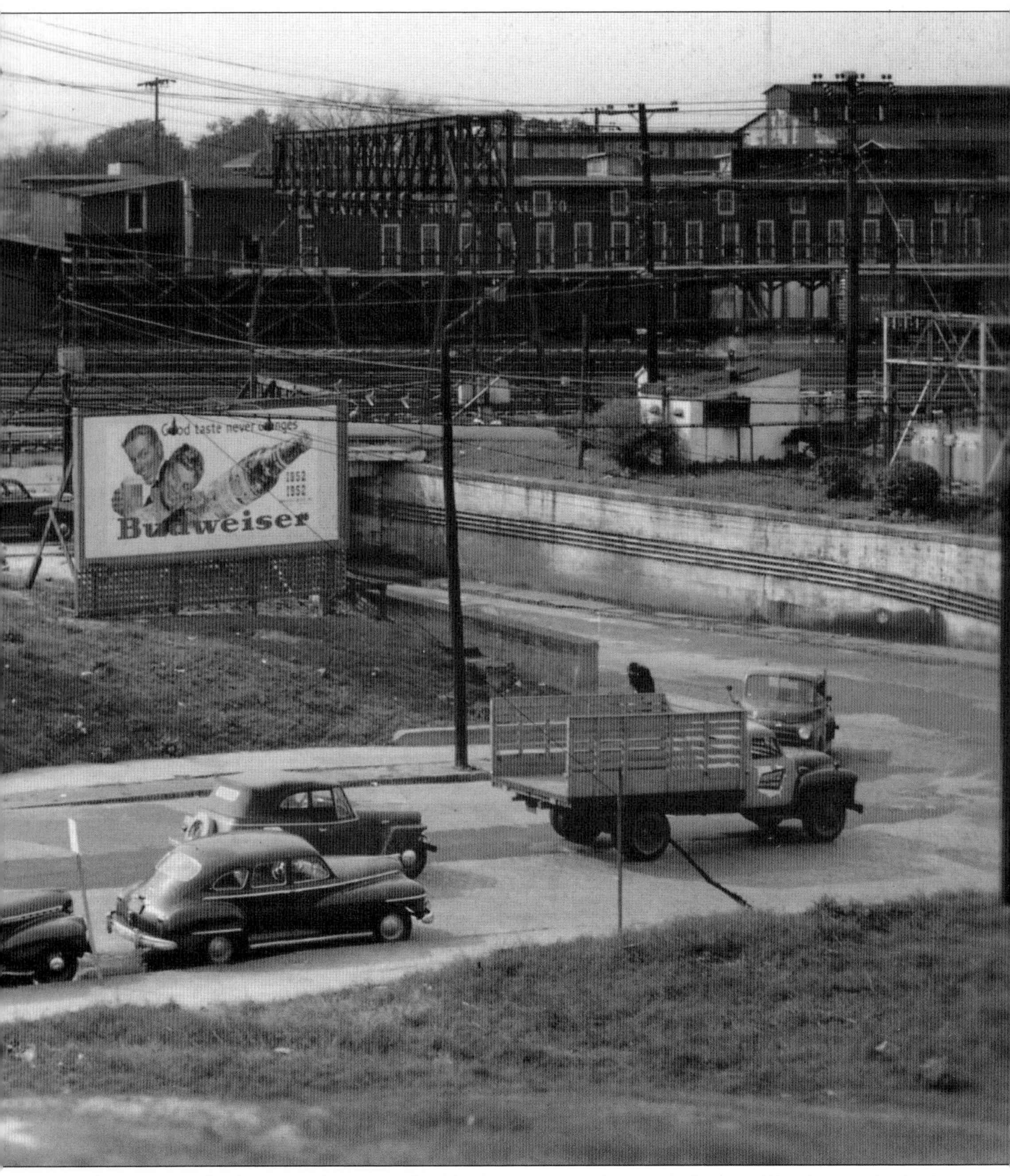

The photograph of the north end of the Myrtle Avenue underpass in Jacksonville shows a Budweiser billboard in the 1950s at a time when Anheuser-Busch became the largest brewer in the United States. To handle the demand for Anheuser-Busch beer, expansion was needed, with its second brewery built in 1951 in Newark, New Jersey. In 1954, its third brewery opened in Los Angeles. By the end of the decade, a fourth brewery opened in Tampa. Also in the photograph is the Atlantic Ice & Coal Company building in the foreground on Dennis Street. (Courtesy of National Archives.)

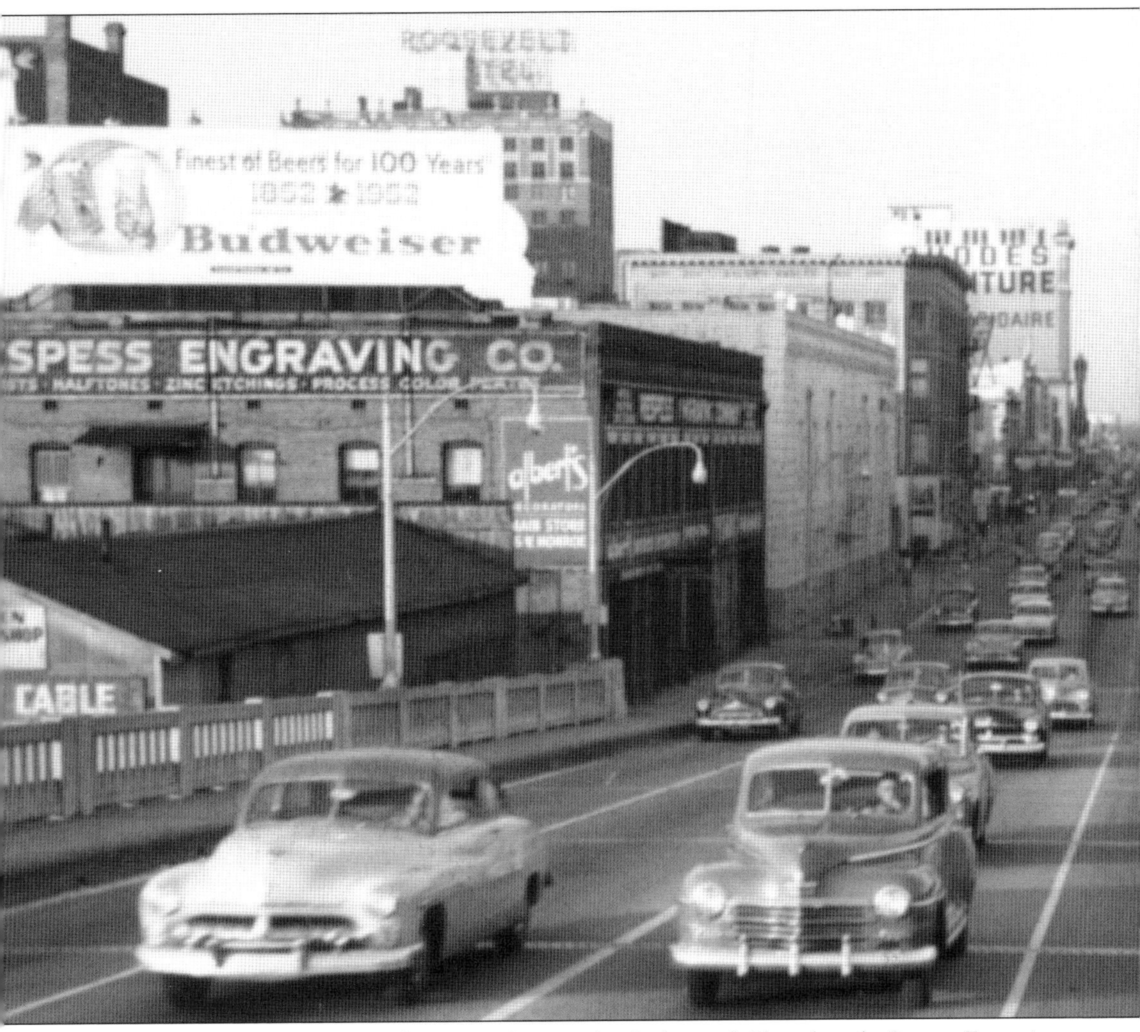

A photograph from 1952 looks north on Main Street with a Budweiser billboard on the Respess Engraving Company building. The billboard celebrates Anheuser-Busch being in business for 100 years as of the photograph's date. The Rhodes Furniture building in the foreground, built in 1914, was demolished in 2002 to make way for the new downtown Jacksonville Public Library. (Courtesy of National Archives.)

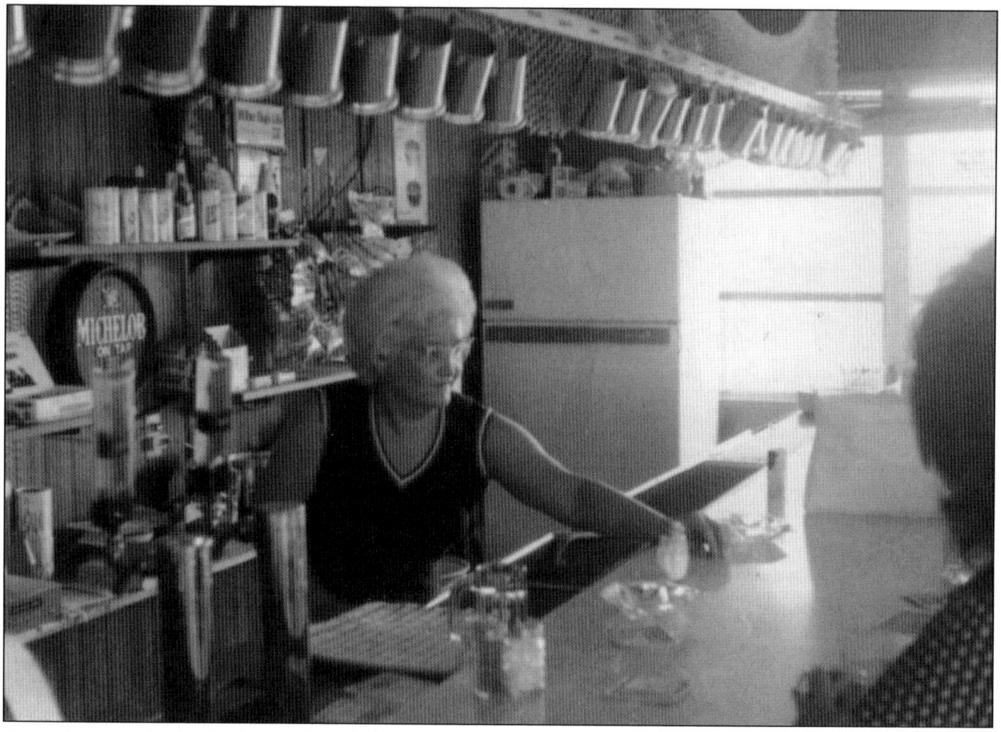

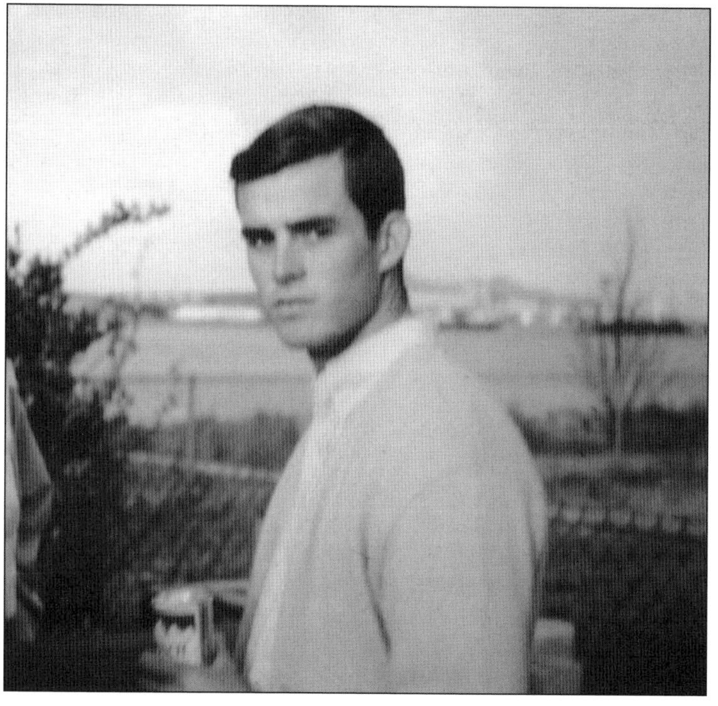

This photograph is of a bartender at the Captains Club bar at Jacksonville Beach in 1972. Behind the bartender is a Michelob sign. Michelob is a pale lager introduced by Anheuser-Busch in 1896. The name "Michelob" comes from the Czech Republic town of Měcholupy, which, in German, was called Michelob when it was once part of Germany. (Courtesy of Beaches Museum.)

Maxey Moody III, a grandnephew of Gustav Muller, drinks a Busch beer at Miller Creek on the St. Johns River with the Mathews Bridge in the background in 1962. Busch beer was introduced in 1955 and is named after August Anheuser "Gussie" Busch Jr., the president and chief executive officer of Anheuser-Busch at the time. From 1955 to 1979, it was called Busch Bavarian Beer. (Courtesy of Andrew R. Nicholas.)

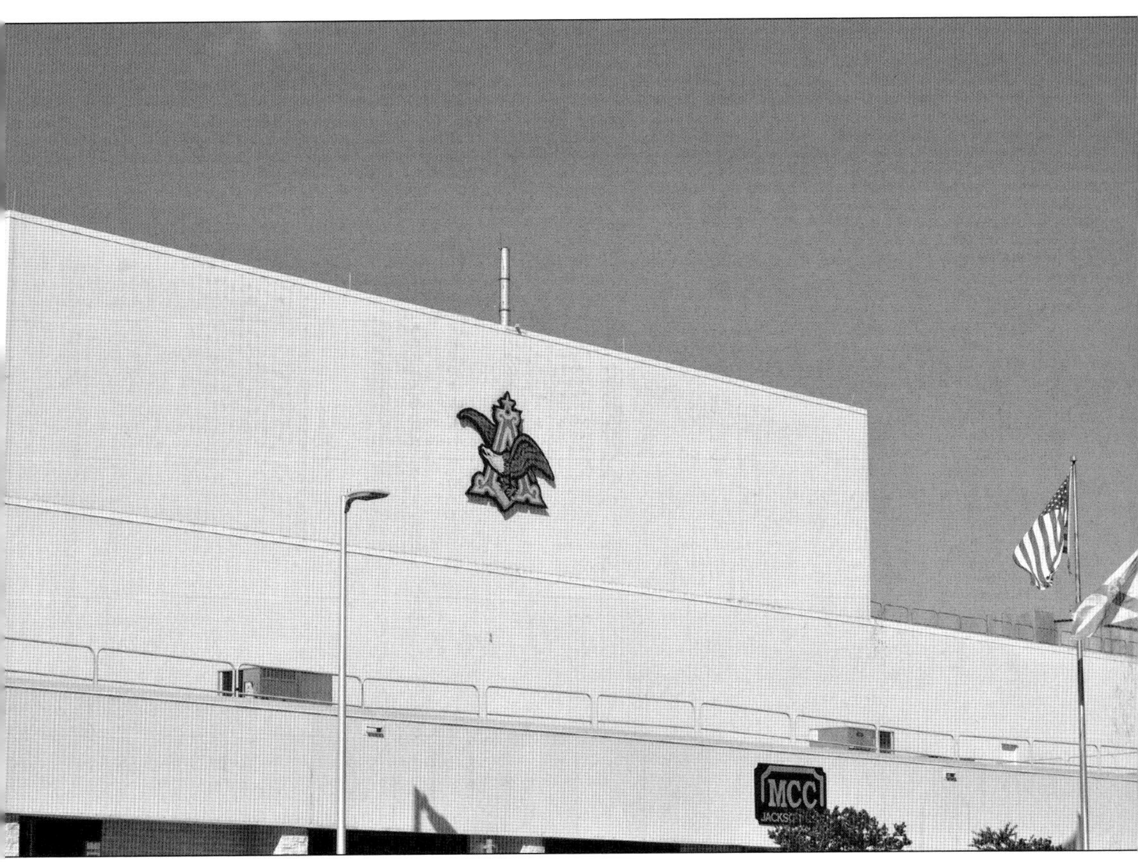

The Metal Container Corporation is an Anheuser-Busch company that manufactures aluminum cans for its breweries. In 1973, the Metal Container Corporation opened a can manufacturing plant on the west side of Jacksonville to mostly serve the Jacksonville Anheuser-Busch plant. At the Jacksonville Metal Container Corporation, 25,000 pounds of aluminum are turned into cans, with two-thirds going to the Jacksonville Anheuser-Busch plant. The photograph shows the exterior of the Metal Container Corporation in 2024. (Courtesy of Andrew R. Nicholas.)

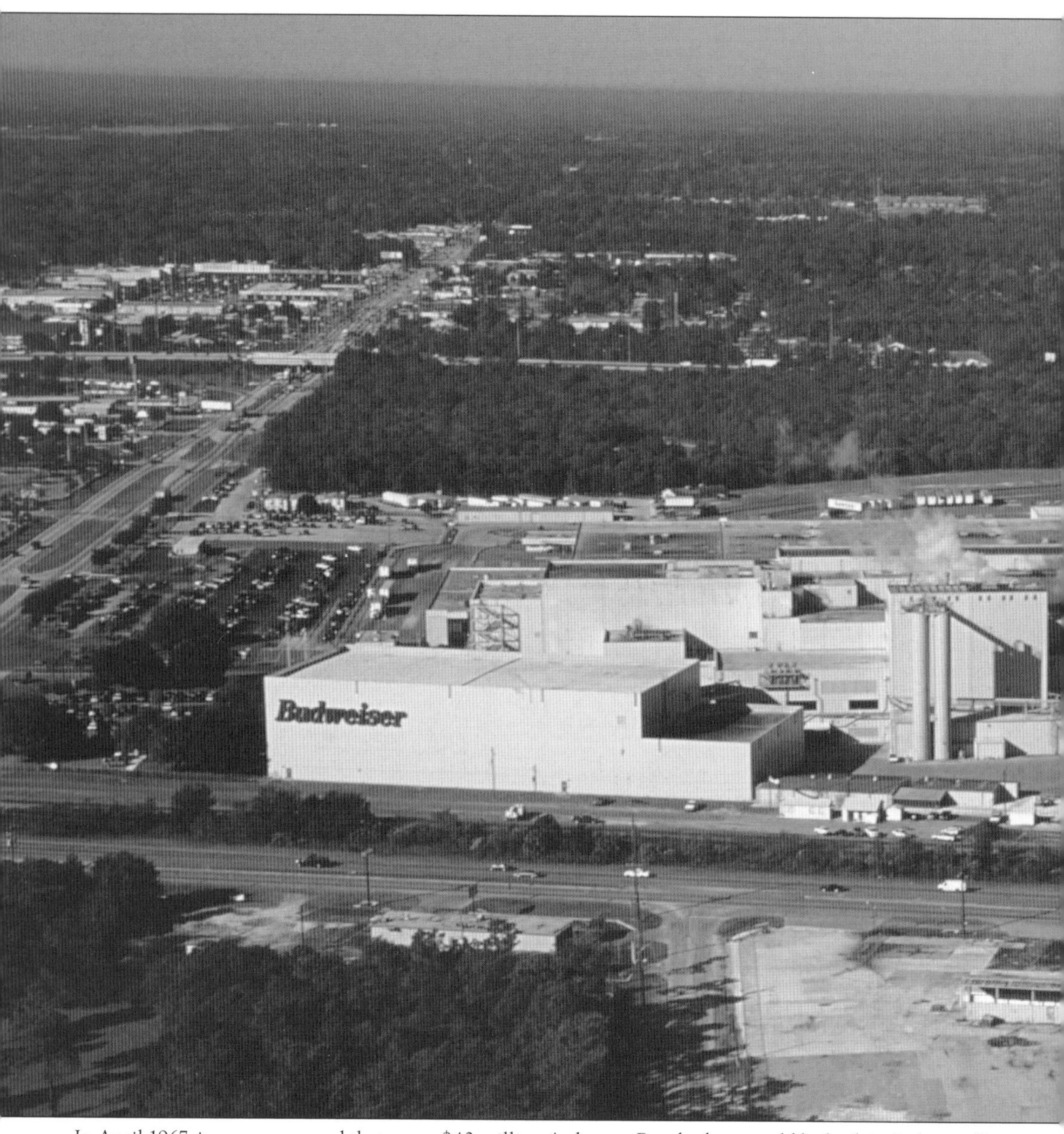

In April 1967, it was announced that a new $40-million Anheuser-Busch plant would be built in Jacksonville on 200 acres on the north side of Main Street. The Jacksonville Anheuser-Busch plant opened in 1969, making Florida the first state to have two Anheuser-Busch plants with one in Tampa. The Jacksonville plant had an initial capacity of 1.1 million barrels of beer per year. After years of expansions, by 2024, the Jacksonville plant was producing over 9 million barrels of beer per year, making it the third-largest

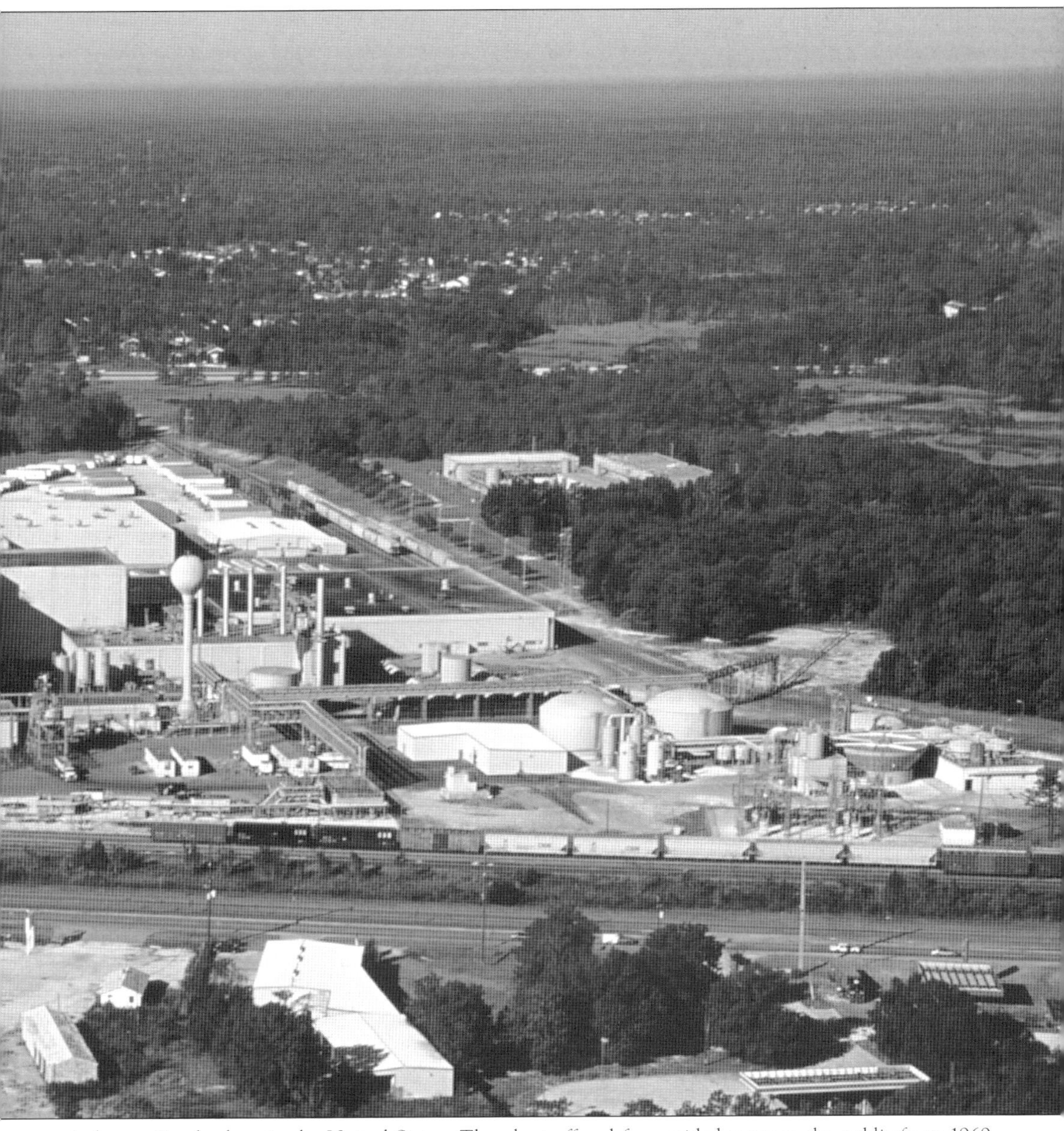

Anheuser-Busch plant in the United States. The plant offered free guided tours to the public from 1969 to 2019. The public could see this Anheuser-Busch beer being brewed and learn how it is made. The aerial photograph shows the Jacksonville Budweiser brewery in the late 1990s. (Courtesy of Lawrence V. Smith, University of North Florida.)

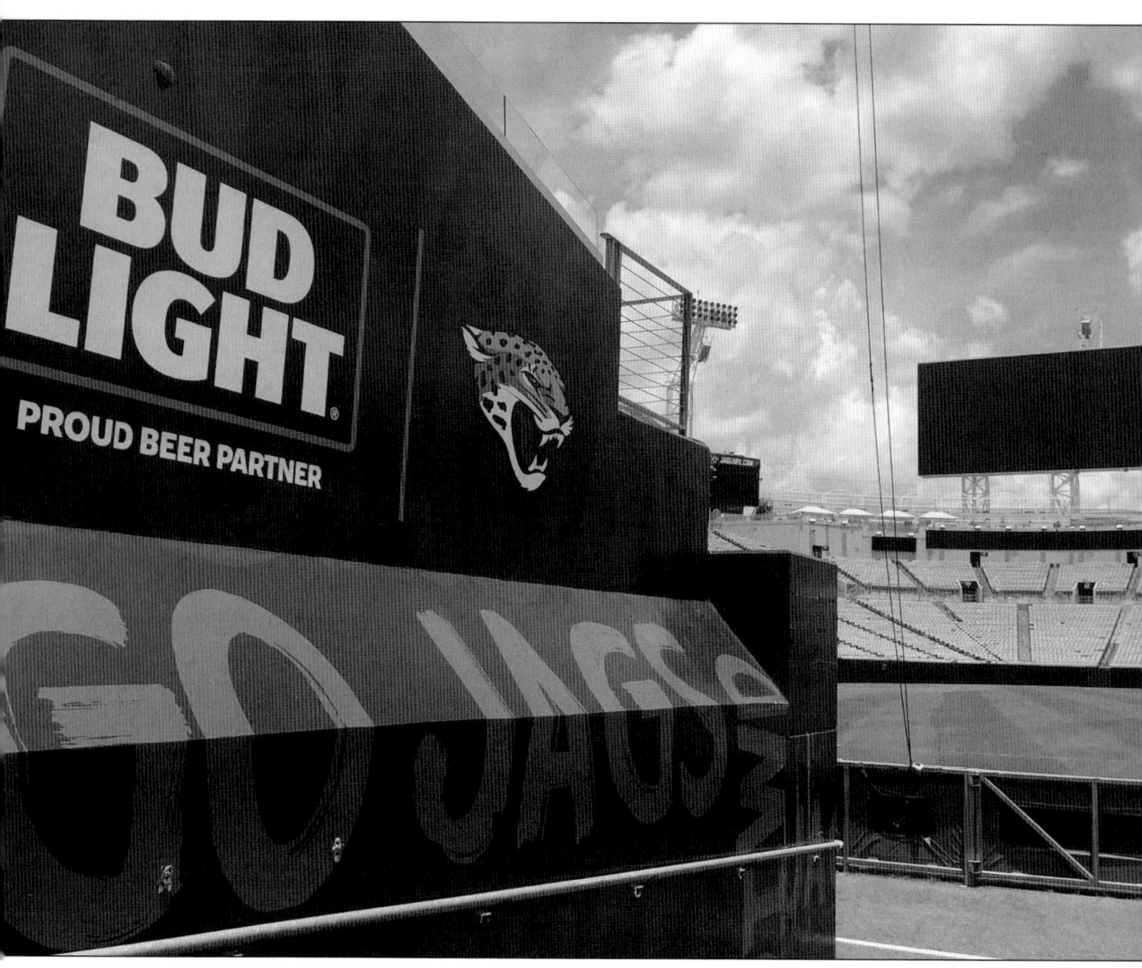

Anheuser-Busch has been a long-standing sponsor of the Jacksonville Jaguars since they first started in 1995. The partnership between Anheuser-Busch and the Jacksonville Jaguars has also established the Bud Light brand as a popular beer for those attending EverBank Stadium. Bud Light was introduced in 1982 as a low-calorie beer to compete with Miller Lite. The photograph from 2023 shows the interior of EverBank Stadium with Bud Light and Jacksonville Jaguars advertising. This publication is not affiliated with or endorsed by the Jacksonville Jaguars. (Courtesy of Andrew R. Nicholas.)

Five

CRAFT OF THE BREWERIES

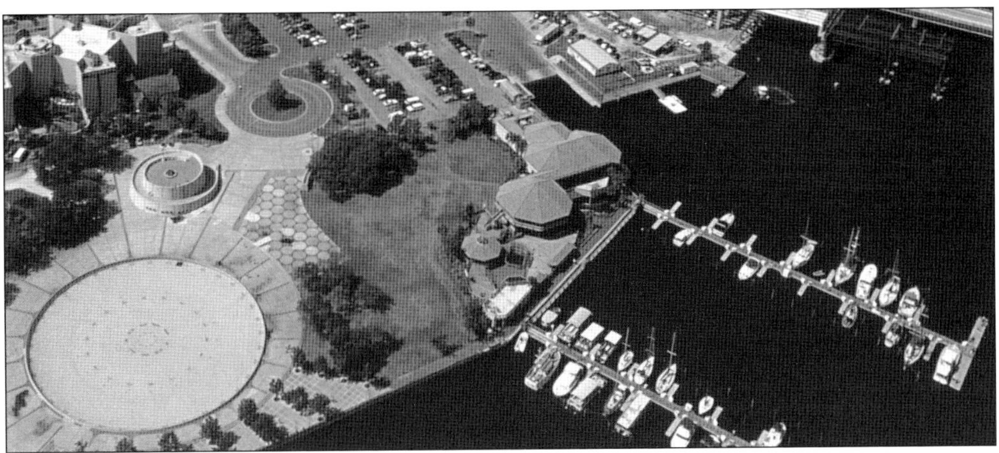

River City Brewing Company opened in 1993 at the former restaurant Harbormasters, seen near the center of the photograph from 1992 with its adjacent marina. Several beers brewed by River City Brewing Company include Acosta IPA, Jackson Pale Ale, and River City Hops IPA. River City Brewing Company closed in 2021 and was demolished the following year to make way for a new apartment complex and restaurant. (Courtesy of Lawrence V. Smith, University of North Florida.)

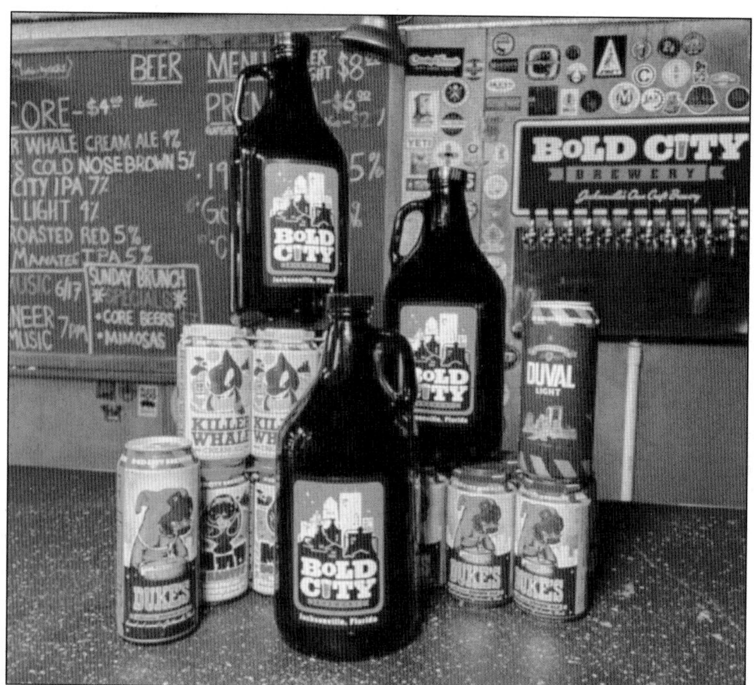

Bold City Brewery was the first craft brewery in Jacksonville, opened in 2008 by Susan Miller and her son Brian Miller. Bold City Brewery's main location opened in 2008 on Rosselle Street, and a taproom and brewery later opened in 2017 on Bay Street. The most popular beers of Bold City Brewery are Duke's Cold Nose Brown Ale, Killer Whale Cream Ale, Mad Manatee IPA, Bold City IPA, and Duval Light lager. (Courtesy of Bold City Brewery.)

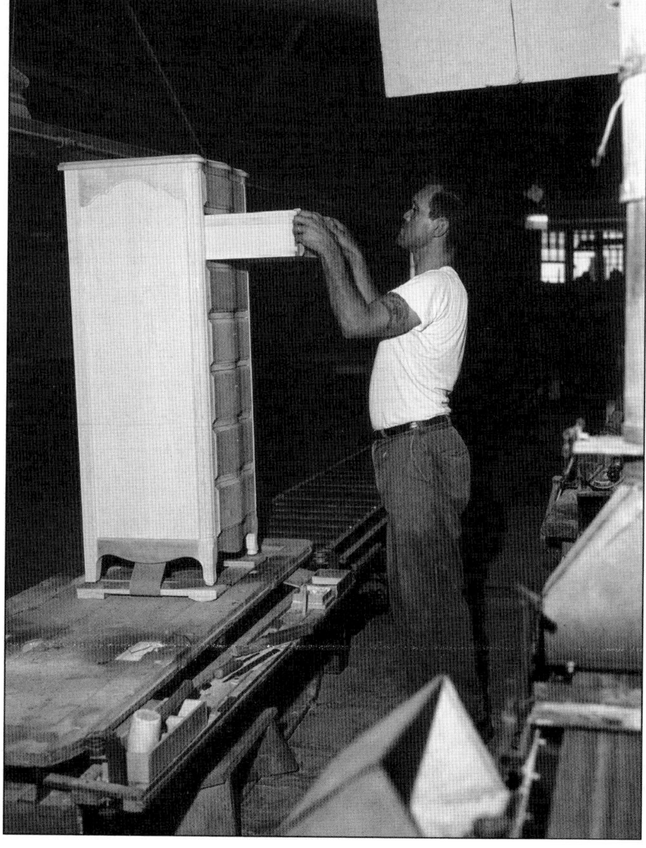

The Schell-Sassee Manufacturing Company operated out of the present-day location of Bold City Brewery in the 1920s. The Dixon Powdermaker Furniture Company later operated out of the warehouse making furniture that was fully made from wood. The photograph shows an employee at Dixon Powdermaker Furniture Company inspecting a newly made dresser in 1967. (Courtesy of State Archives of Florida.)

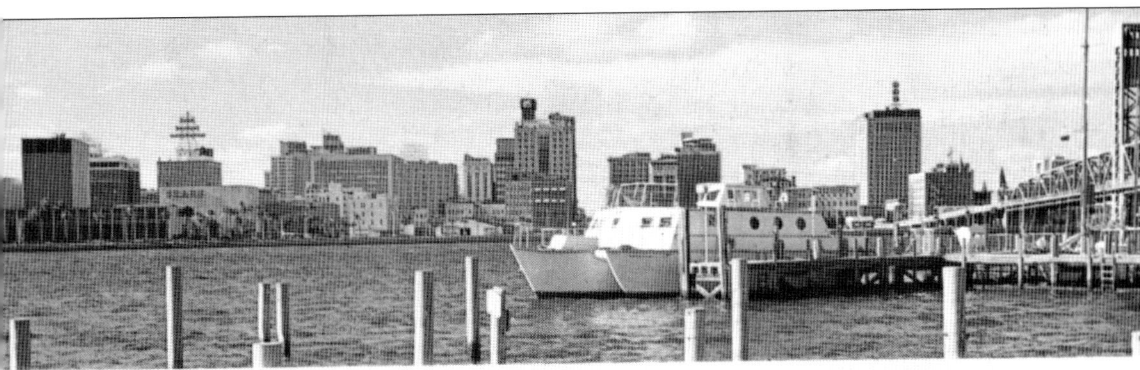

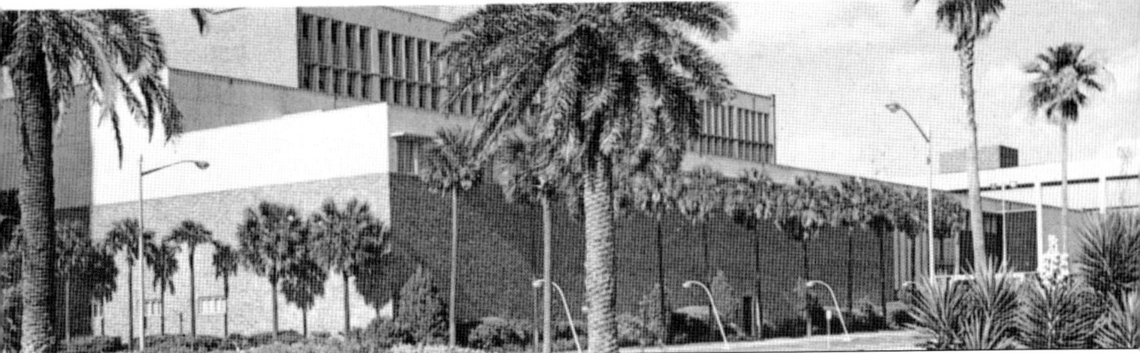

The origin of the nickname "Bold City" goes back to 1968. Jacksonville was given the nickname "Bold New City of the South" after it merged with Duval County that year to create a consolidated government entity. The postcard from 1968 shows downtown Jacksonville along with its new slogan "The Bold New City." (Courtesy of Digital Commonwealth Massachusetts Collection Online.)

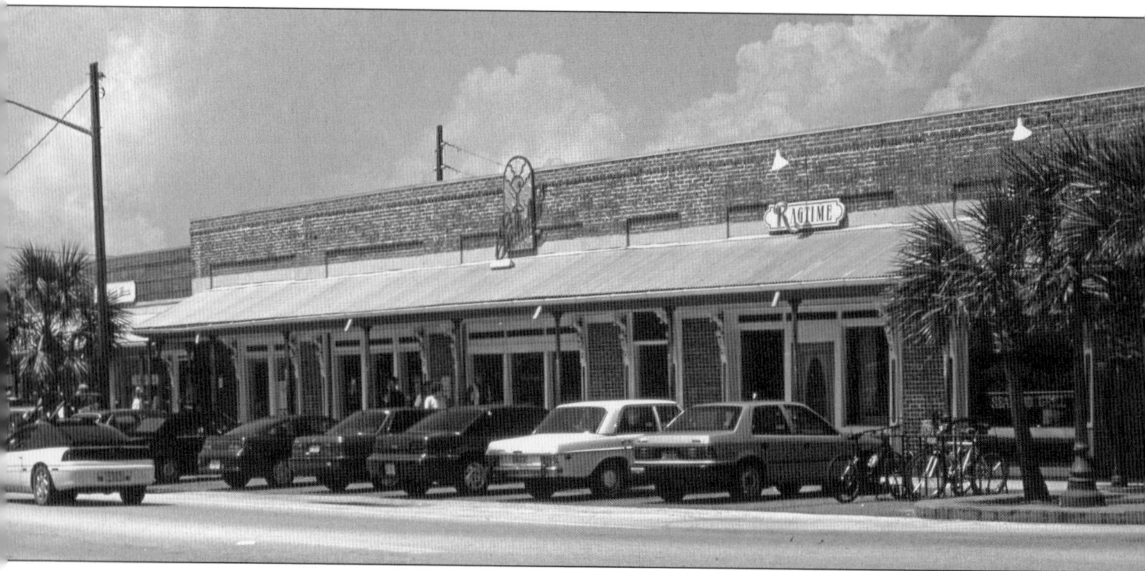

Ragtime Tavern was opened in 1983 in Atlantic Beach by brothers Tom Morton and Bill Morton. In 1990, the tavern expanded with a taproom and lounge. In 1994, the restaurant added a microbrewery, making it the first microbrewery in the Jacksonville area. Beers brewed by Ragtime Tavern included Dolphin's Breath Lager, First Coast IPA, and Red Brick Ale. The photograph shows Ragtime Tavern in 1995 on Atlantic Boulevard in Atlantic Beach. In January 2025, Ragtime Tavern permanently closed. (Courtesy of State Archives of Florida.)

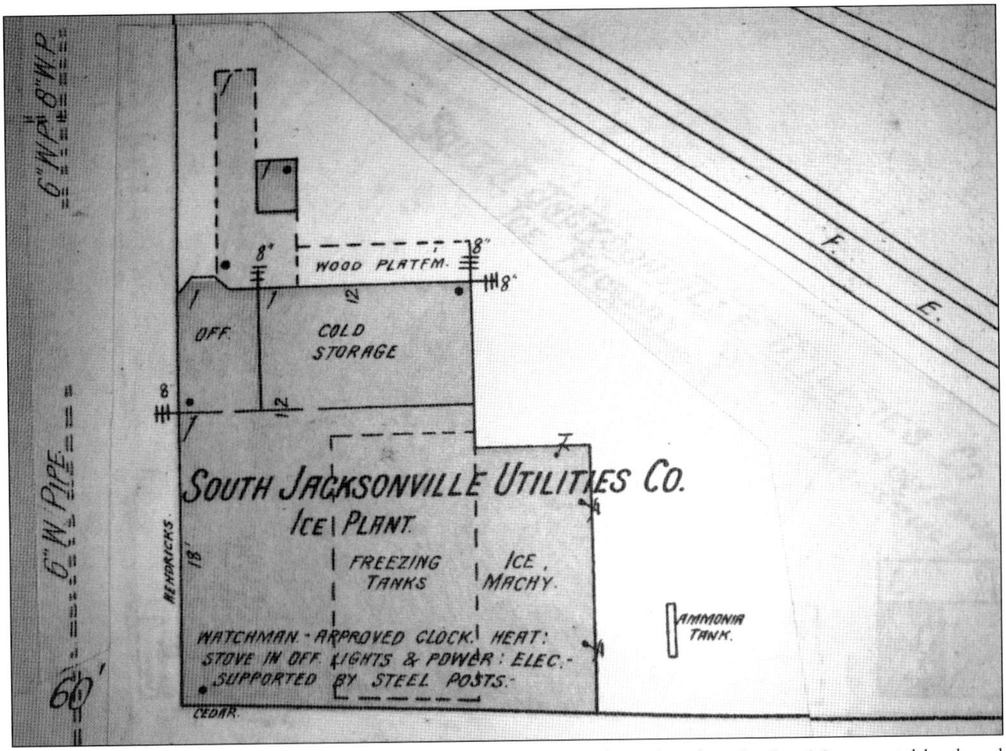

In 1927, a building was constructed on Hendricks Avenue near the railroad in the San Marco neighborhood for use as ice storage for the South Jacksonville Utilities Company. The Sanborn Fire Insurance Company map from 1927 shows the building as South Jacksonville Utilities Co. Ice Plant. In 1954, the Moyer Marble & Tile Company used the building as a warehouse. It later added a showroom and stayed here until the early 2000s. (Courtesy of Jacksonville Public Library.)

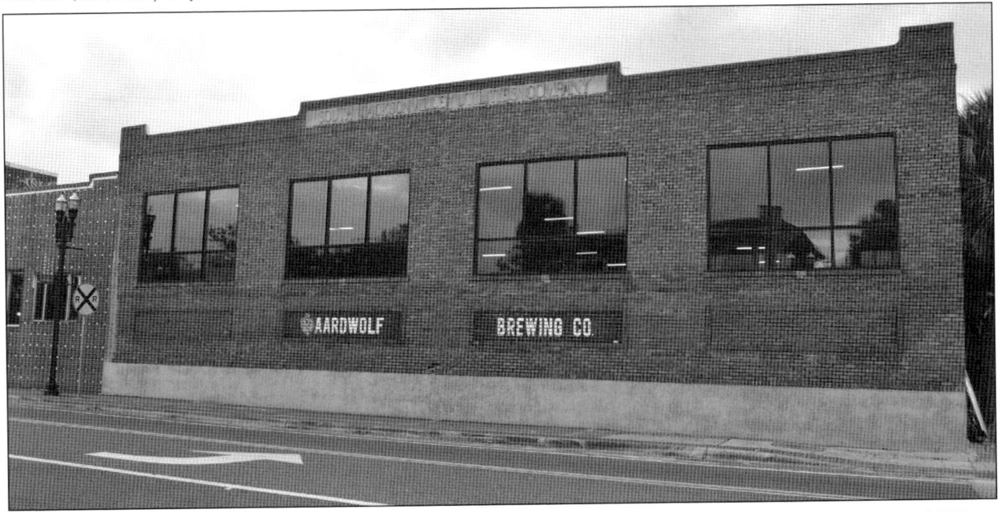

Aardwolf Brewing Company was founded by Preben Olsen and Michael Payne, opening in 2013 in the former South Jacksonville Utilities Company building. Beers brewed by Aardwolf Brewing include Southbank IPA, Alvin's Coffee Brown ale, Slowking lager, Styrofoam Pony stout, Little Hans lager, Belgian Pale Ale, and Nonchalant IPA. An aardwolf is a hyena-like carnivore that lives in southern and eastern Africa. (Courtesy of Andrew R. Nicholas.)

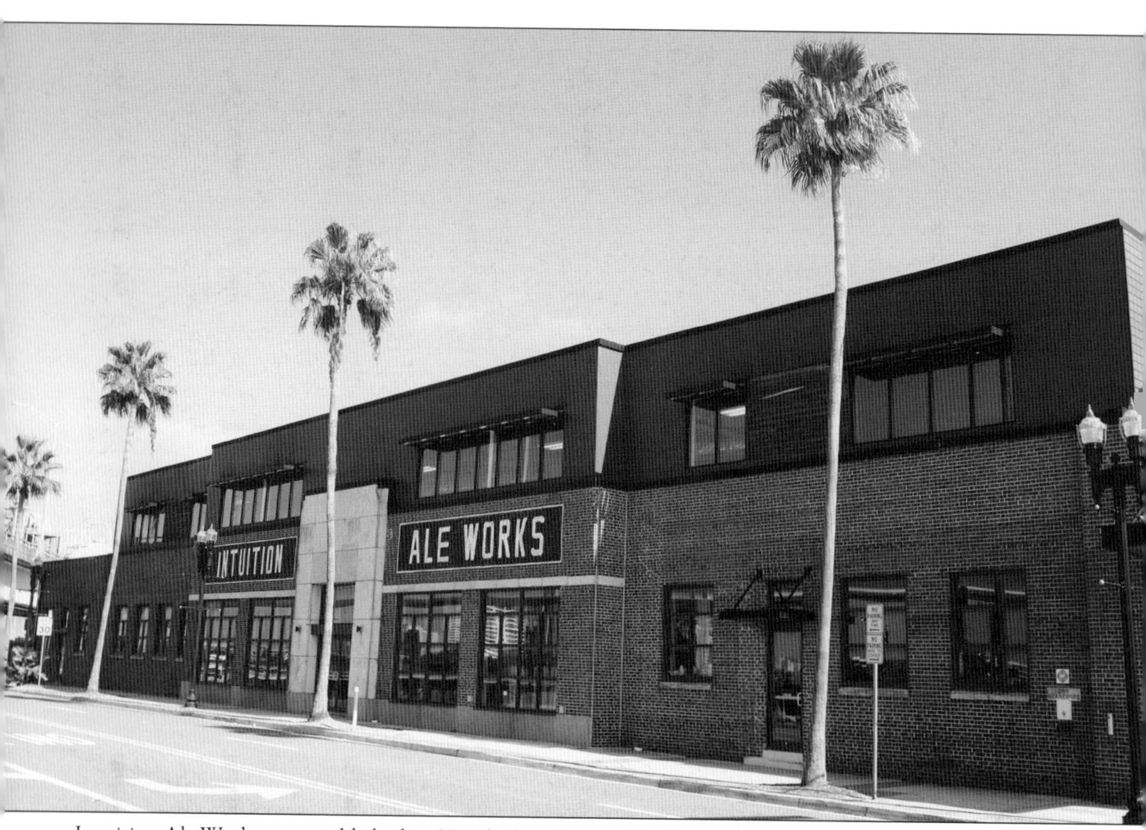

Intuition Ale Works was established in 2010 by local brewer Ben Davis on King Street. Intuition Ale Works is the first Florida-based craft brewery to can its own beer. In 2016, Intuition Ale Works closed its King Street location and moved to a newly renovated building at 929 East Bay Street complete with a rooftop beer garden, taproom, and brewery. Roughly half of 929 East Bay Street is occupied by Intuition Ale Works, while the other half is a distillery called Manifest Distilling. Beers brewed by Intuition Ale Works include People's Pale Ale, I-10 IPA, Jon Boat Coastal Ale, Easy on the Eyes IPA, Party Wave hazy IPA, King Street Stout, Wheelhouse Brown ale, and Shrimp Boat Kölsch. (Courtesy of Andrew R. Nicholas.)

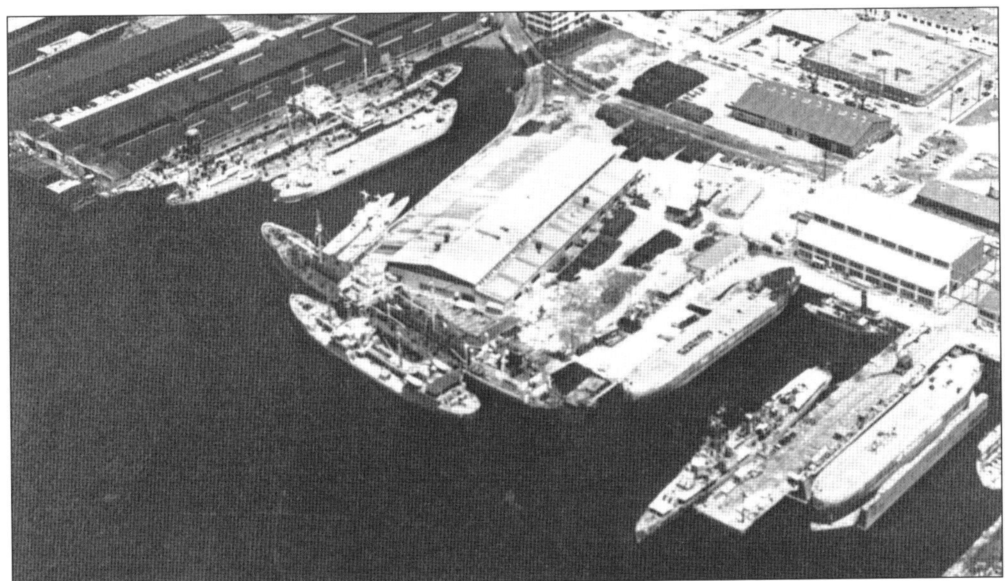

This is an aerial photograph from the 1950s featuring 929 East Bay Street, the square-like building in the upper-right corner. Near 929 East Bay Street are the Jacksonville shipyards, which, in the previous decade, were busy with building Liberty ships in World War II. The shipyards in the photograph before World War II were the Merrill-Stevens Dry Dock & Repair Company. (Courtesy of State Archives of Florida.)

In 2019, Intuition Ale Works opened the Bier Hall, a 6,000-square-foot music venue at 929 East Bay Street. Bands that have played at the Bier Hall include Of Montreal, the Mountain Goats, Jenny Lewis, and Yonder Mountain String Band. The photograph shows the local Jacksonville band Folk Is People performing at the Bier Hall in 2022. (Courtesy of Bill Delaney.)

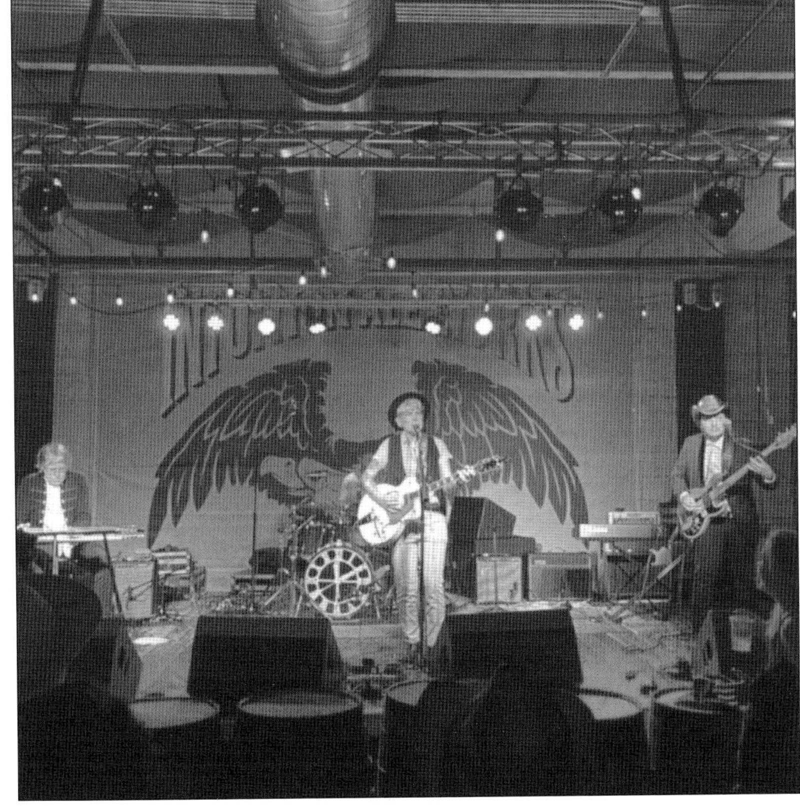

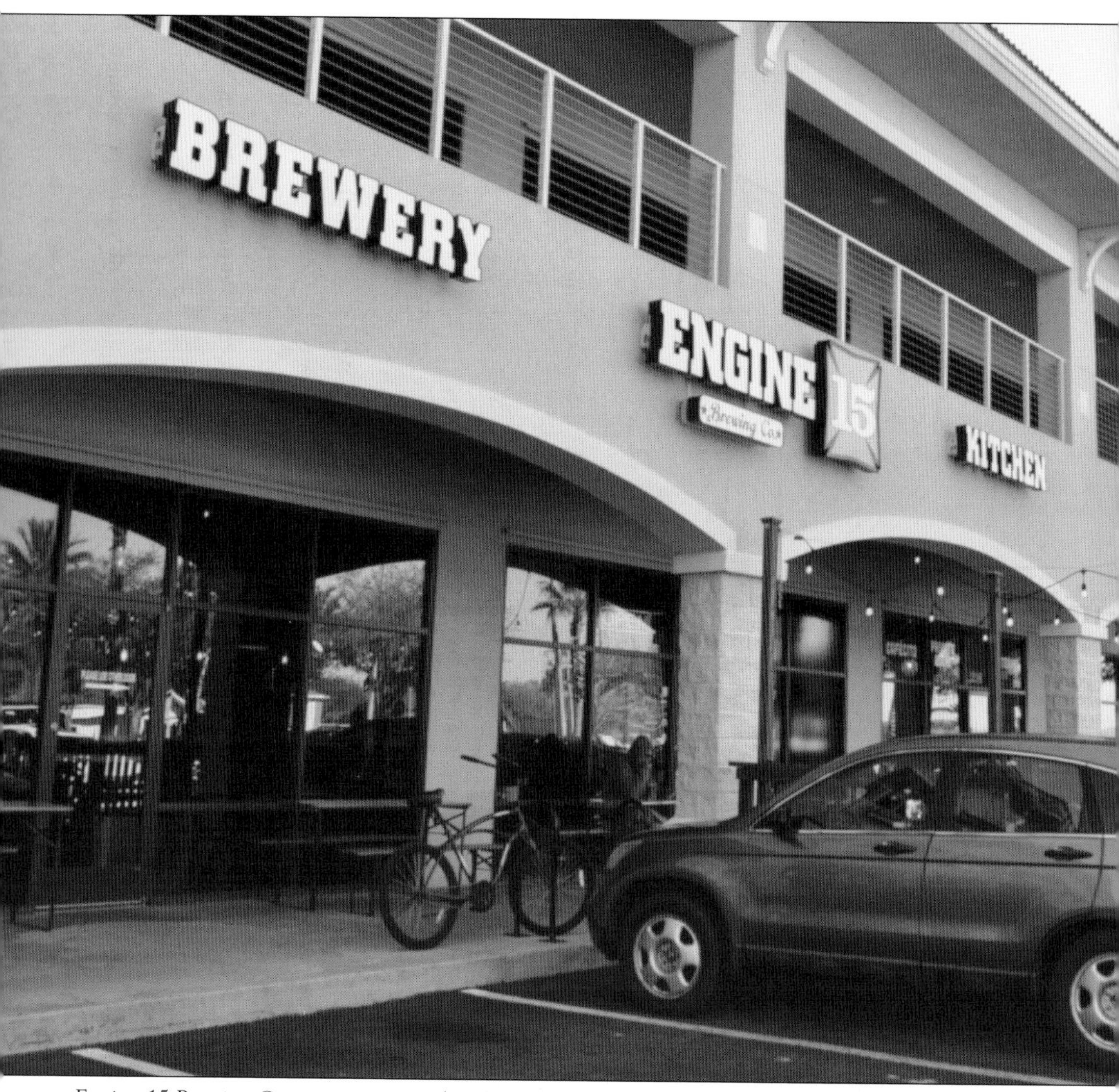

Engine 15 Brewing Company originated with Jacksonville locals Luciano Scremin's homebrewing in the late 2000s and Sean Bielman's knowledge of brewery operations. Jacksonville, around 2010, had a lack of craft beers, which gave Scremin and Bielman the idea of starting their own craft brewery. In 2010, Engine 15 Brewing Company renovated a brewery and eatery at a shopping center in Jacksonville Beach. In 2014, Engine 15 Brewing Company acquired a building complex on Myrtle Avenue, which it renovated to become a taproom and larger brewery space. Engine 15 Brewing Company's second location on Myrtle Avenue permanently closed in 2020. Beers brewed by Engine 15 include J'ville Lager Beer, Nut Sack Double Brown Ale, Galaxy Quest IPA, The Empire Did Nothing Wrong imperial stout, Double Drop, Sunday Funday Session IPA, Oscar's Oatmeal Stout, Captain A-Hop IPA, and 904 Weissguy wheat beer. The name "Engine 15" comes from a 1962 Ford fire truck owned by Luciano Scremin. (Courtesy of Andrew R. Nicholas.)

Veterans United Craft Brewery was opened in 2013 by a group of American veterans organized by US Navy veteran Ron Gamble to produce and enjoy craft beer. Beers brewed by Veterans United include HopBanshee IPA, Wackey Badger Hazy IPA, Scout Dog 44 altbier, Fish Camp pilsner, Raging Bonde golden ale, and Buzzin' Bee honey rye wheat ale. (Courtesy of Veterans United Craft Brewery.)

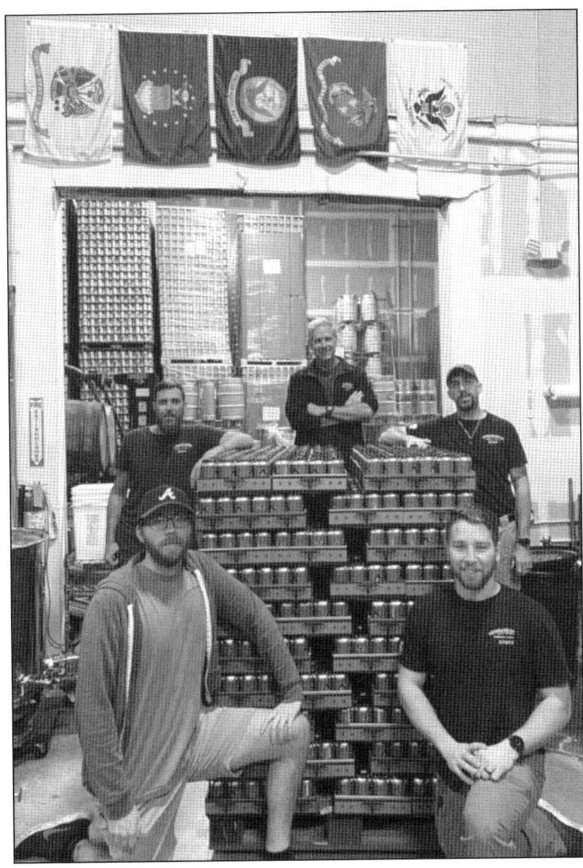

Wicked Barley Brewing Company was opened in 2016 on Goodbys Creek off Baymeadows Road by Tobin Turney, Brett Baker, Philip Maple, and Bradley Suefloh. Beers brewed by Wicked Barley Brewing include Left Leg pale lager, Geoffrey stout imperial, Blood Drive orange-flavored IPA, Brierwood brown ale, and The Eradicator double IPA. This photograph shows a Wicked Barley Brewing employee giving a tour of the brewery in 2023. (Courtesy of Verance Photography and Wicked Barley Brewing.)

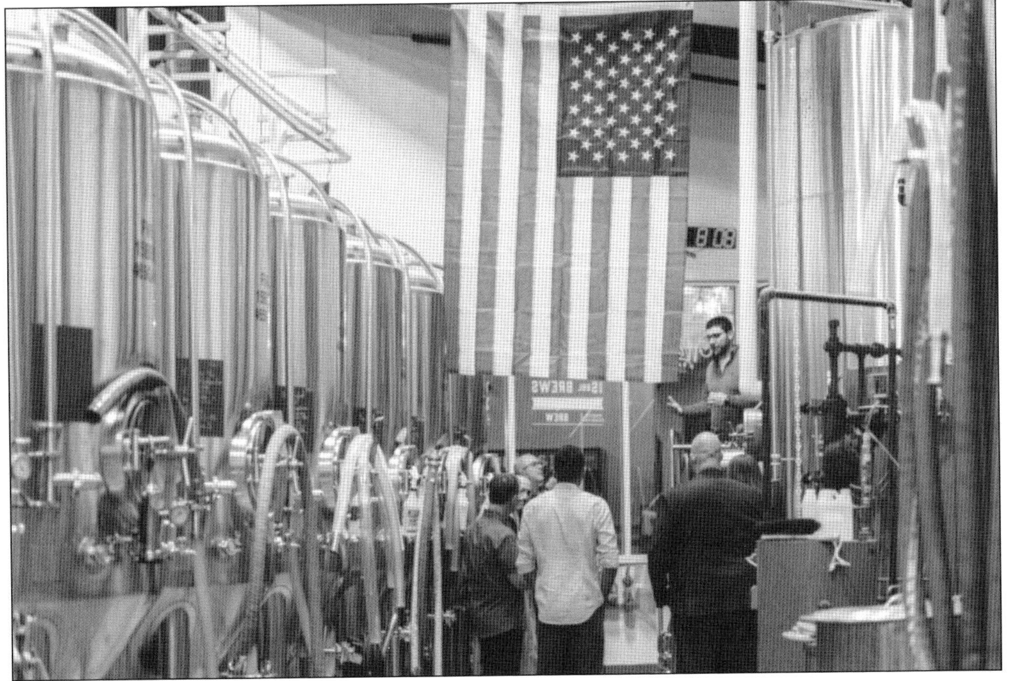

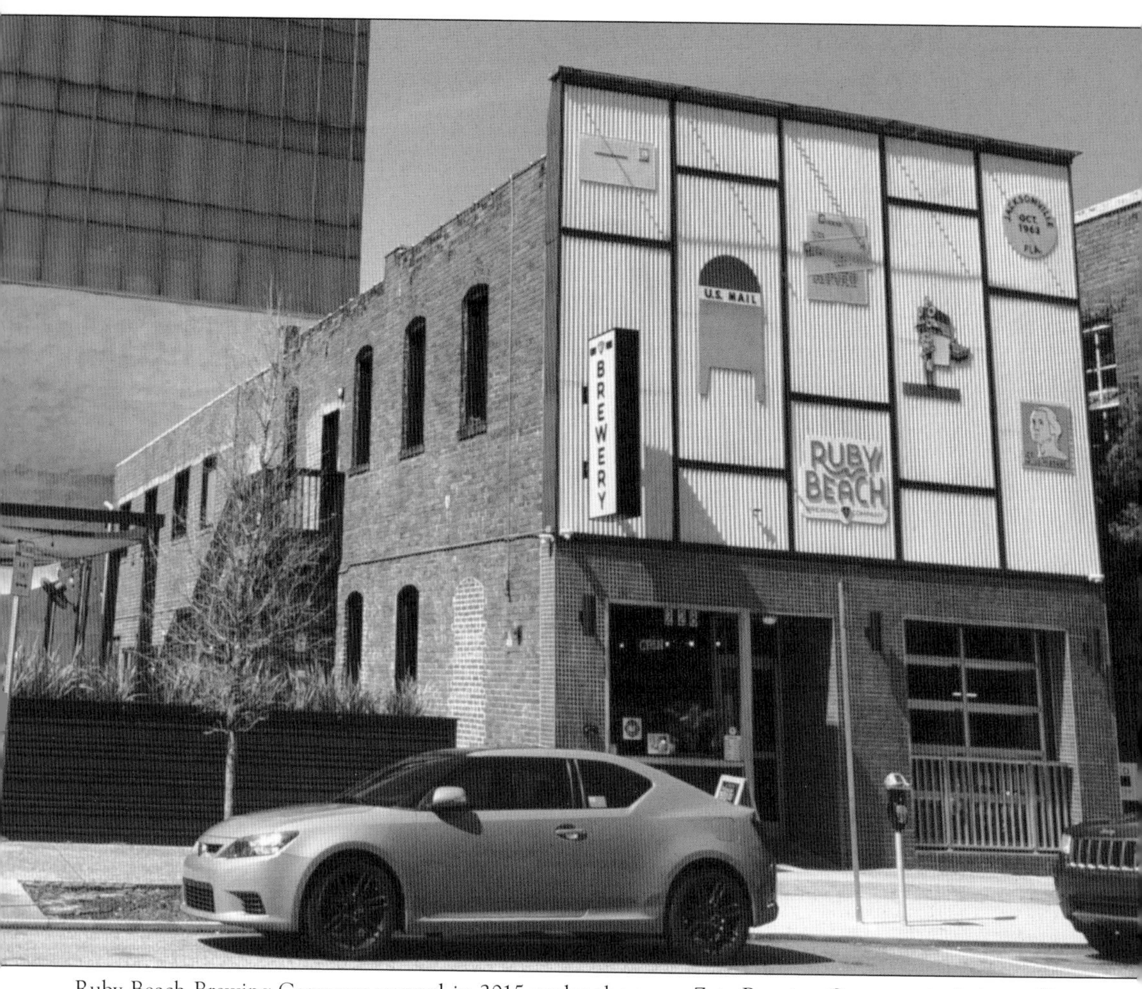

Ruby Beach Brewing Company opened in 2015 under the name Zeta Brewing Company in Jacksonville Beach as a brewery and restaurant. In 2018, Zeta Brewing Company removed the restaurant element of the business to focus more on the brewery itself in addition to renaming itself Ruby Beach Brewing Company. In 2020, Ruby Beach Brewing Company relocated from Jacksonville Beach to the newly renovated Letter Shop building, dating to 1905, at 228 East Forsyth Street in downtown Jacksonville. From 1945 to 2004, the Futch Letter Shop occupied the building, inadvertently giving the building its name. From 2010 to 2017, the Letter Shop building was occupied jointly by a messenger tote bag manufacturer called Burro Bags and a record store called Budget Records. Beers brewed by Ruby Beach Brewing Company include a sour called Scallywag, Twin Finn pale lager, and an IPA, American Garage. The photograph shows Ruby Beach Brewing Company and various postal service signs on the front of the building in 2023. (Courtesy of Andrew R. Nicholas.)

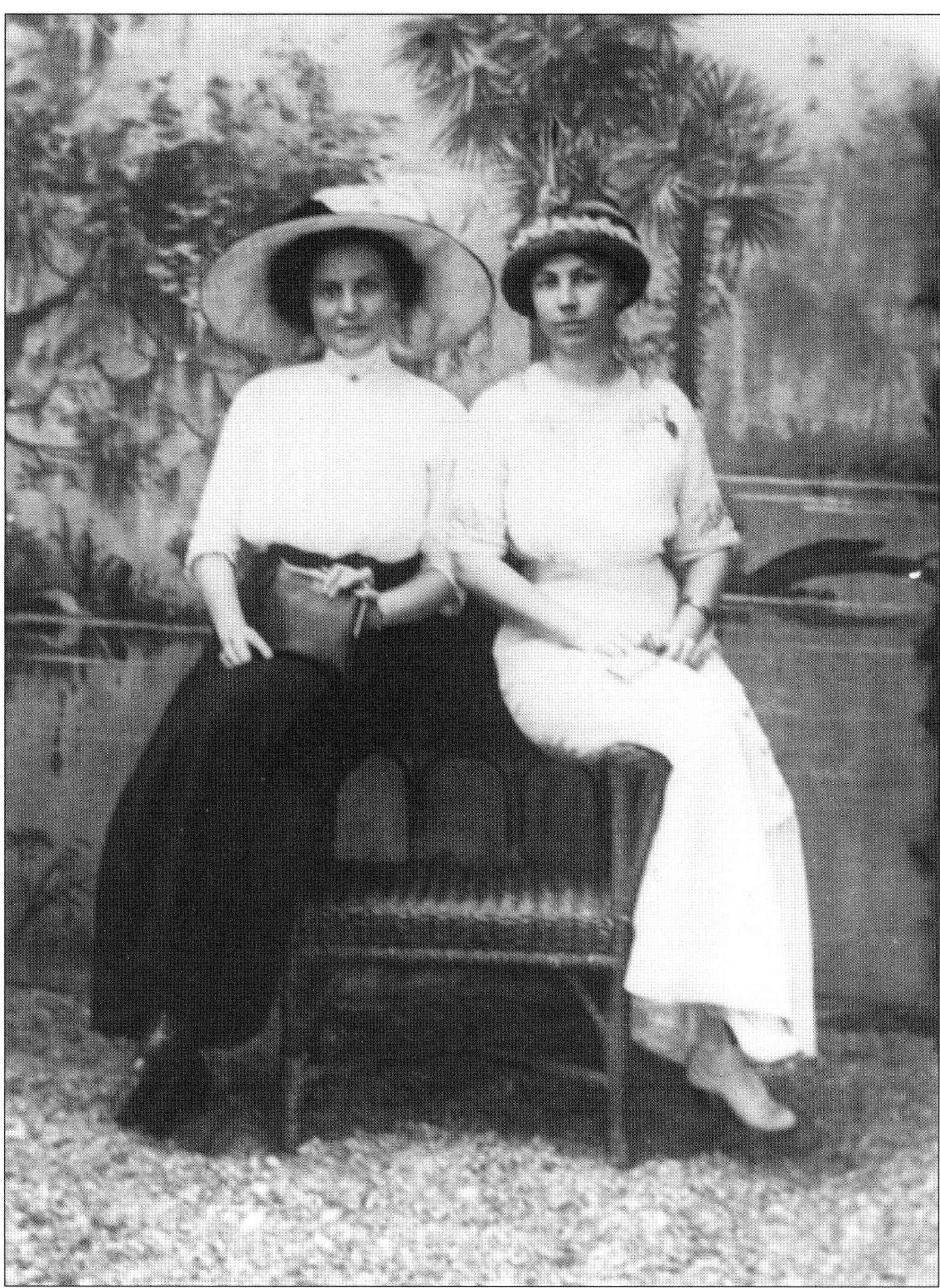

William Edward Scull, a civil engineer and surveyor, and his wife, Eleanor, set up a tent at present-day Jacksonville Beach in 1884 to survey the area for the coming Jacksonville & Atlantic Railroad. Eleanor set up a general store and post office in the area. The small settlement that grew out of the Sculls' work was named Ruby after their daughter, Ruby Scull. A town followed soon thereafter, and on May 13, 1886, Ruby was renamed Pablo Beach. On June 15, 1925, Pablo Beach became Jacksonville Beach. (Courtesy of Beaches Museum.)

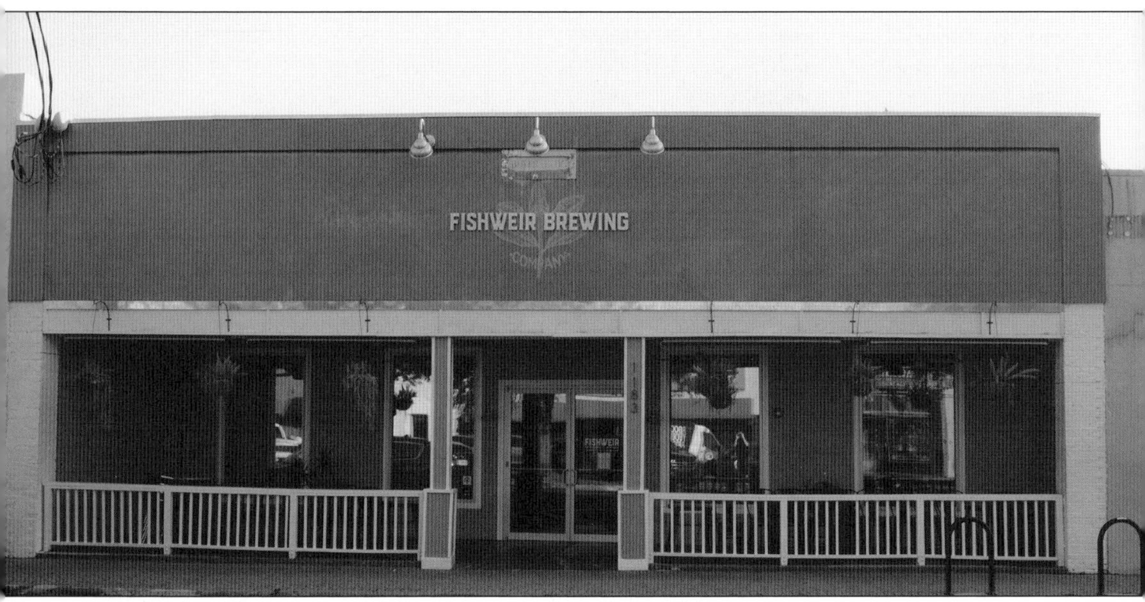

Fishweir Brewing Company opened in 2018 on Edgewood Avenue in the Murray Hill neighborhood. Jacksonville local homebrewer Broc Flores and his wife, Stacey Flores, renovated a former nightclub called Fat Kat and turned the space into Fishweir Brewing Company. In 2021, Fishweir Brewing Company further renovated behind the building and made it into a beer garden called The Backyard. Beers brewed by Fishweir Brewing Company include Lazy River pilsner, King of the Hill hazy IPA, Big Fishweir West Coast IPA, Take Me To Your Liter IPA, Bait and Switch coffee blonde, and First Block saison. The photograph shows the exterior of Fishweir Brewing Company in 2023. (Courtesy of Andrew R. Nicholas.)

Fishweir Brewing Company is named after Fishweir Park, which is named after nearby Fishweir Creek. Big Fishweir Creek and Little Fishweir Creek are both tributaries of the St. Johns River. The photograph shows a group of girls walking along Fishweir Creek in the 1920s. (Courtesy of Jacksonville Historical Society.)

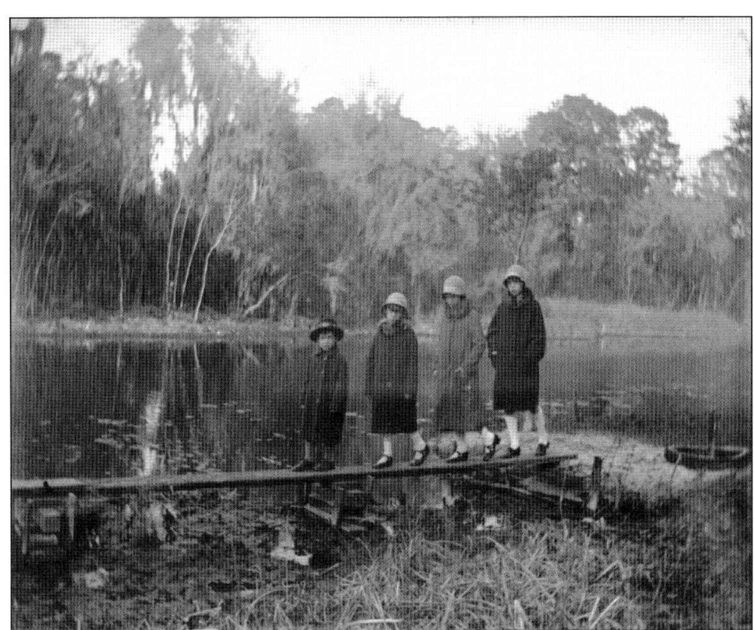

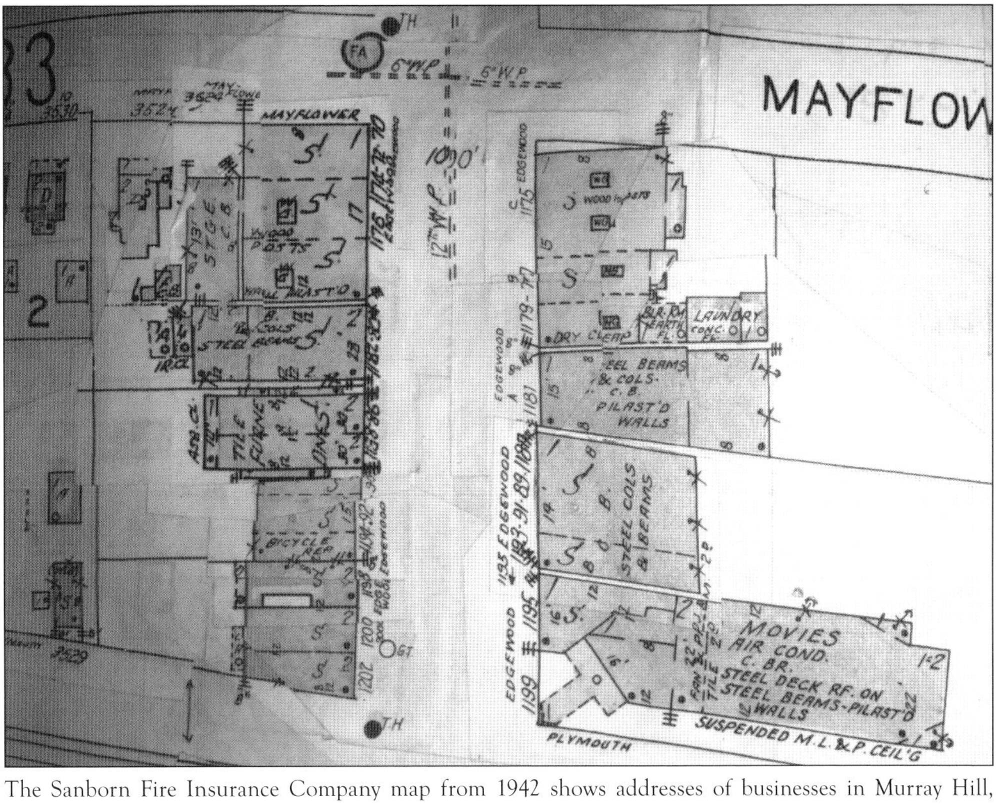

The Sanborn Fire Insurance Company map from 1942 shows addresses of businesses in Murray Hill, including 1181 Edgewood Avenue, now 1183 Edgewood Avenue, where Fishweir Brewing Company is located. The building that Fishweir Brewing Company now occupies, in the center, among other restaurants and bars in the immediate area, dates to 1942. The road running through the center is Edgewood Avenue. (Courtesy of Jacksonville Public Library.)

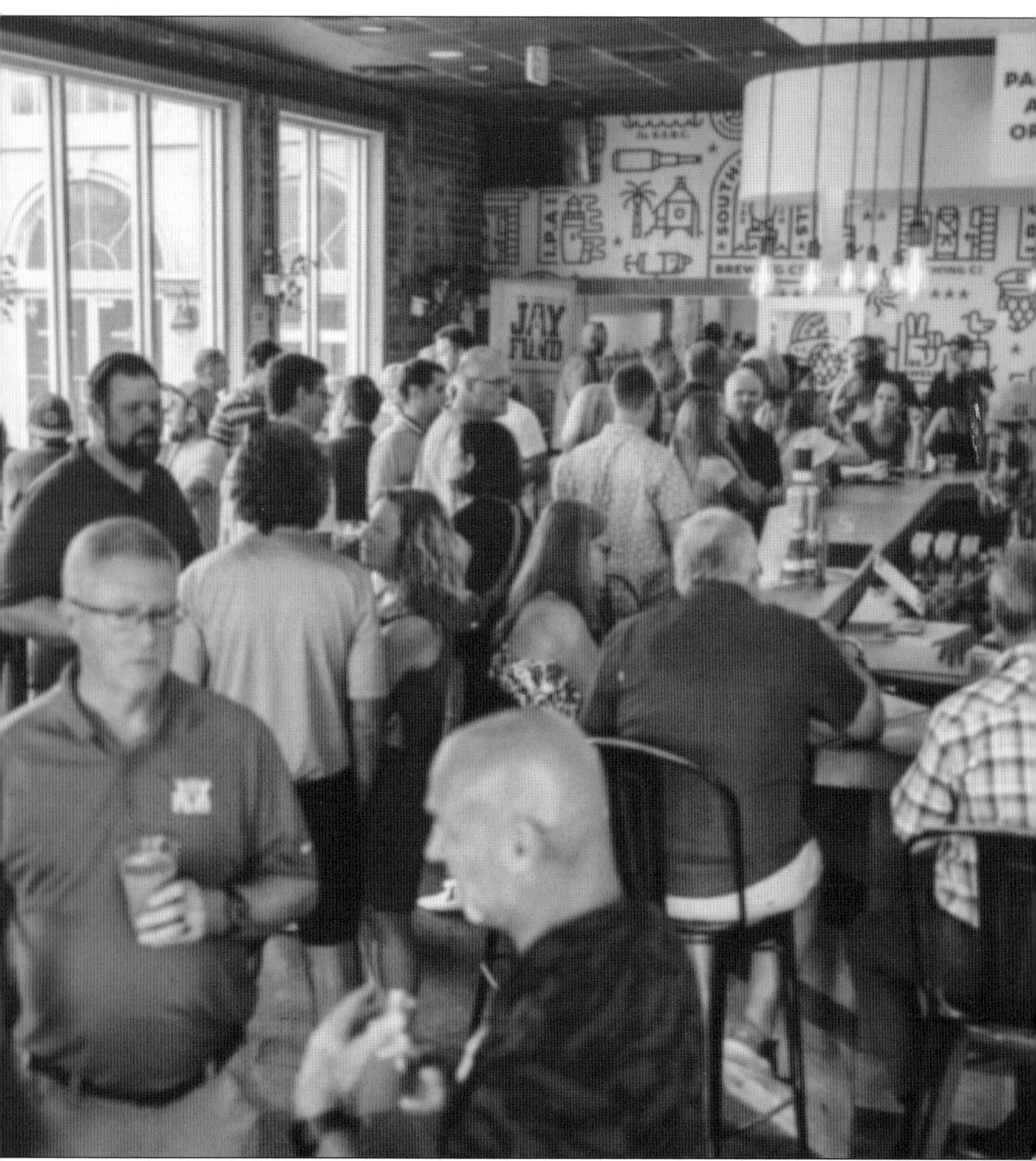

Rhode Island natives Corey Adams and Jay Varney turned their passion for homebrewing into reality by opening Southern Swells Brewing Company in 2016. Southern Swells Brewing occupies a 7,500-square-foot space at Beach Plaza in Jacksonville Beach. Beers brewed by Southern Swells include Karate in the Garage IPA, Endless Summer farmhouse ale, The Longroad Less Traveled porter, and 14 Killstripes sour. (Courtesy of Southern Swells Brewing Company.)

Main & Six Brewing Company was opened on Main Street in 2017 by homebrewer Dennis Espinosa and permanently closed in March 2020 due to the economic impacts of the COVID-19 pandemic. In 2020, Main & Six's imperial stout with a Mexican chocolate variant called Weapons of Mash Destruction won a gold medal award in the chocolate or cocoa beer category at the Best of Craft Beer Awards awarded by the Great American Beer Festival. (Courtesy of Main & Six Brewing Company.)

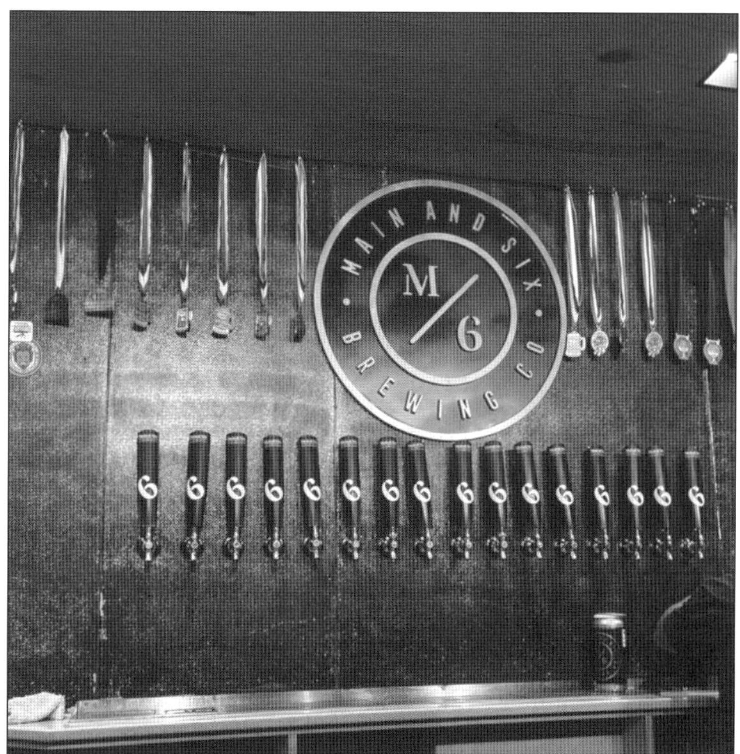

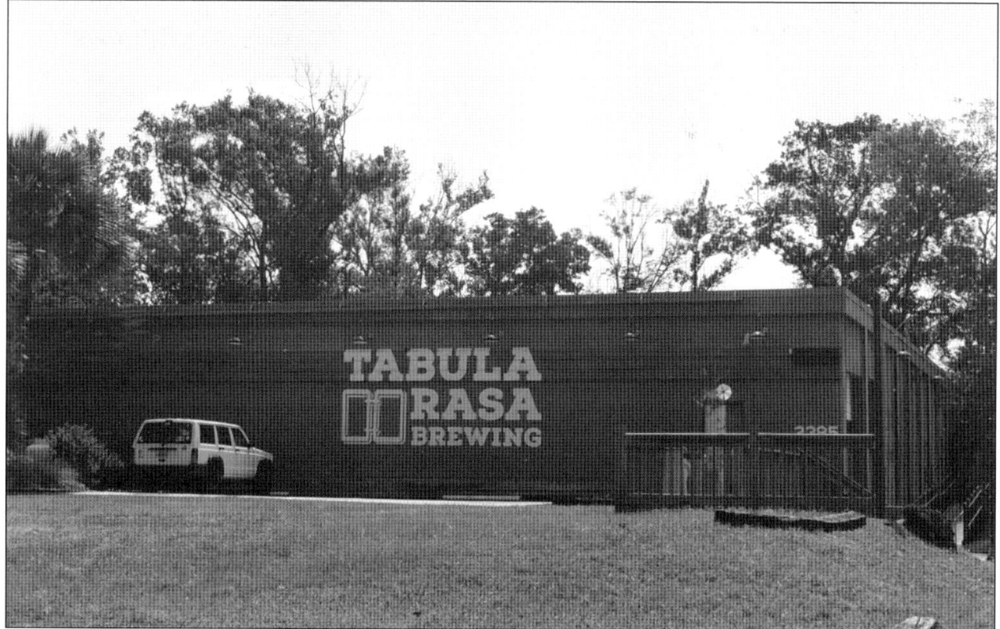

Tabula Rasa Brewing Company was opened in 2018 in the Mixon Town neighborhood by homebrewers Randy Peterson, Jackie Peterson, and Ryan Peterson. The brewery opened at a warehouse on Corbett Street that was built in 1952. Beers brewed by Tabula Rasa included One Ping Only New England IPA, Crazy Mona Coconut Porter, Scarlet Ibis IPA, and The Tartanic Scottish ale. In 2023, Tabula Rasa Brewing Company permanently closed after five years in operation. (Courtesy of Andrew R. Nicholas.)

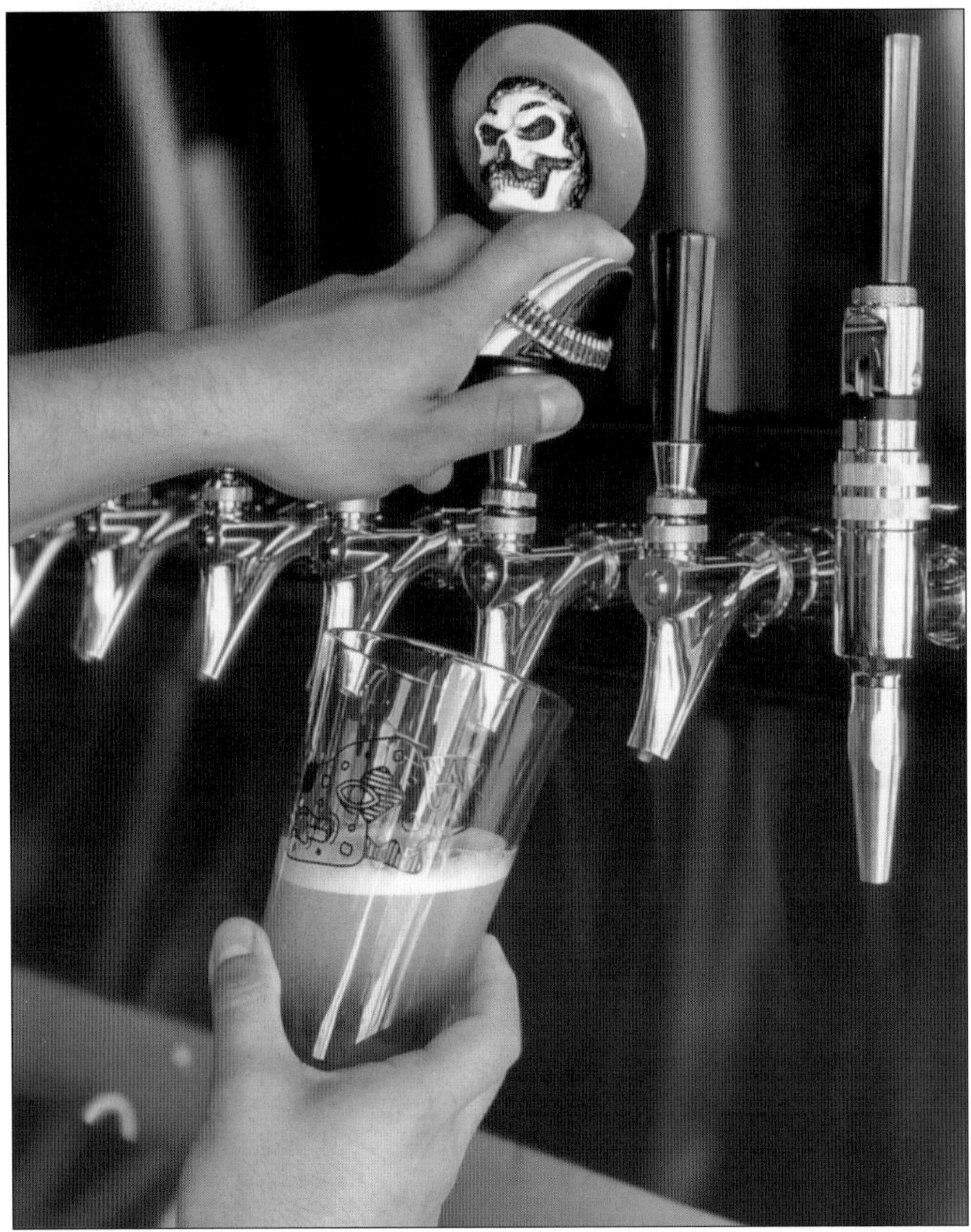

Tepeyolot Cerveceria was opened on Kings Avenue in 2021 as a brewery and restaurant by Luis Melgarejo. It initially began as a food truck in 2020 until the Kings Avenue building was fully renovated to open as a brewery and restaurant. Melgarejo chose the name to honor his Mexican heritage. The photograph shows a bartender pouring a lager out of the Mexican-themed tap handle at Tepeyolot Cerveceria. (Courtesy of Tepeyolot Cerveceria.)

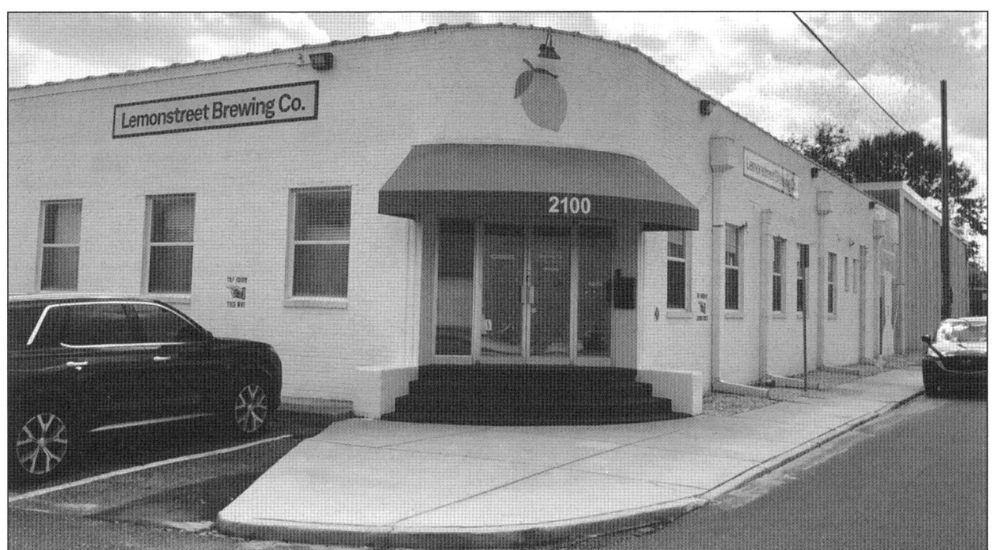

Lemonstreet Brewing Company was opened in 2019 by Joaquin "Joe" Baez and his wife, Maryn, at the corner of Dennis and Lemon Street in the Rail Yard District. Lemonstreet Brewing Company occupied a 20,000-square-foot building erected in 1952. Beers brewed by Lemonstreet included Batholomeow imperial stout, Inconthievable IPA, and Noc Bac IPA. In December 2023, Lemonstreet Brewing permanently closed due to rising global inflation and the lingering effects of the COVID-19 pandemic. (Courtesy of Andrew R. Nicholas.)

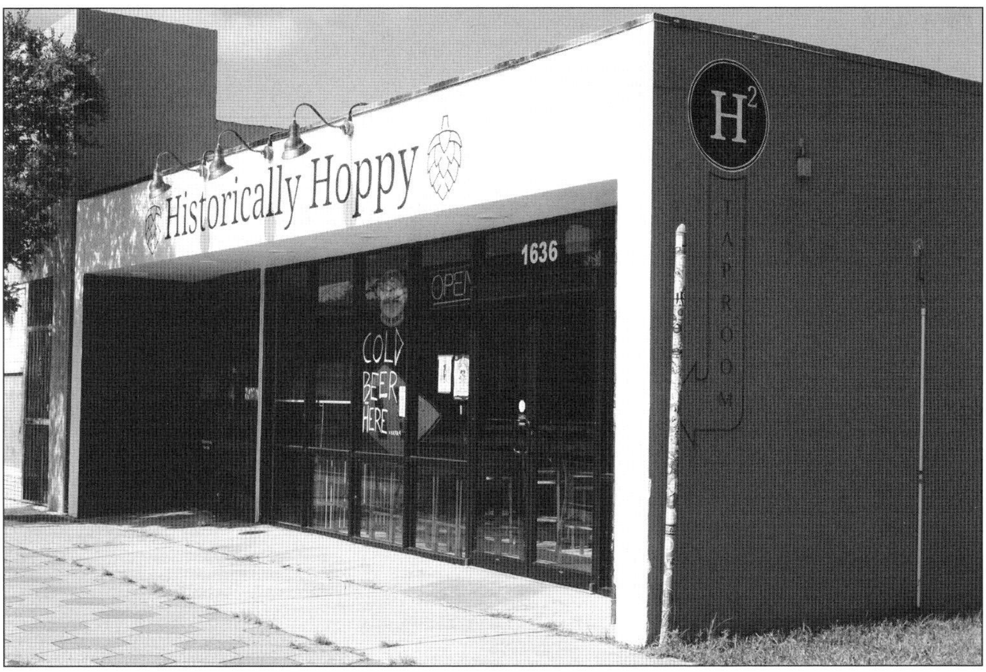

Historically Hoppy Brewing Company was founded in 2022 in the Springfield neighborhood by residents Ryan McFarland, Brianna McFarland, Aaron Leedy, and Natalie Leedy. Beers brewed by Historically Hoppy included Whitty Wheat ale, Farmhouse ale, K&M lager, Eastside IPA, The New Normal West Coast IPA, and the Tipsy Brown Ale. The photograph shows the front of Historically Hoppy in 2024. In October 2024, Historically Hoppy permanently closed. (Courtesy of Historically Hoppy.)

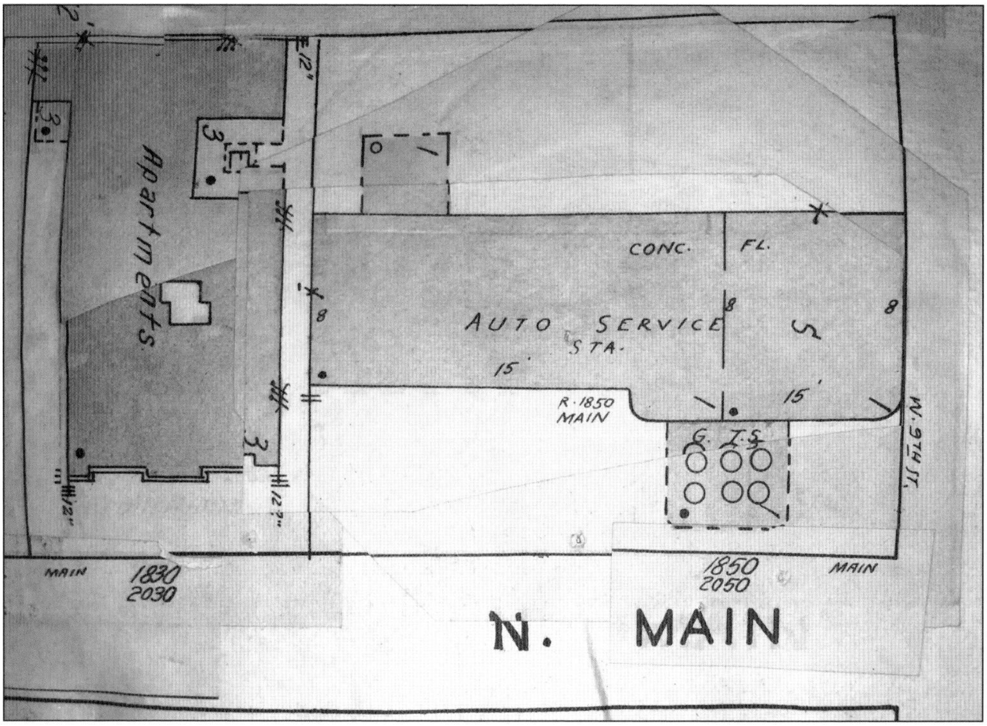

The building at 1850 Main Street in the Springfield neighborhood dates to 1938, when it was first used as an automotive service station by Firestone. In 2003, Firestone sold the building to a developer that converted it into a restaurant called Henrietta's, which was foreclosed in 2009. This Sanborn Fire Insurance Company map from 1942 shows the automotive service station, called Auto Service on the building. (Courtesy of Jacksonville Public Library.)

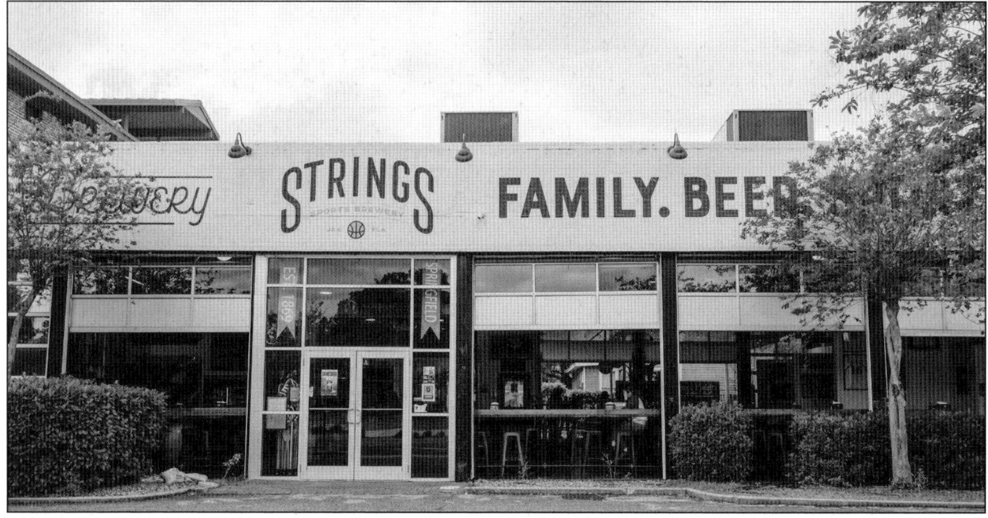

The sports-themed Strings Sports Brewery was opened in 2019 at 1850 Main Street by Scott "Strings" Adeeb and the Adeeb family. Beers brewed by Strings Sports Brewery include String Music lager, Bullet Bob hazy IPA, One Six hazy IPA, Red Caps red ale, and Section 215 blonde ale. In 2024, the former Terry's Country Store in Jacksonville Beach was converted into Strings Sports Brewery's second location. (Courtesy of Strings Sports Brewery.)

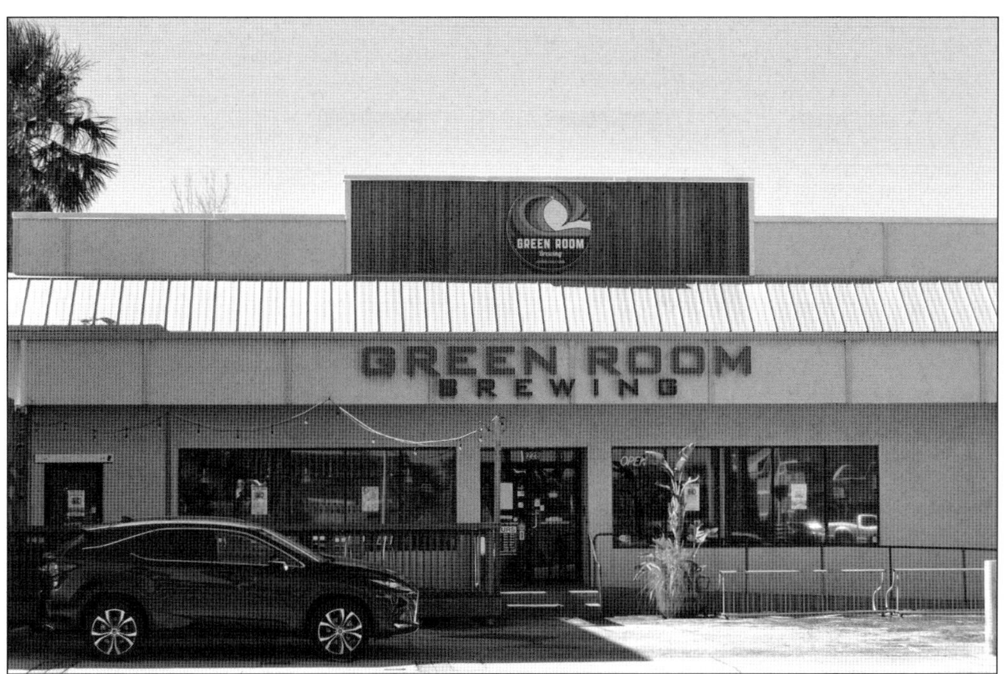

Green Room Brewing was opened in 2011 by Mark Stillman and Eric Luman as Jacksonville Beach's first microbrewery. Beers brewed by Green Room Brewing include Head High IPA, Double Overhead double IPA, Diamond Blueberry blonde, Pablo Beach pale ale, Count Shakula stout, and Quetzalcoatl Imperial red ale. (Courtesy of Andrew R. Nicholas.)

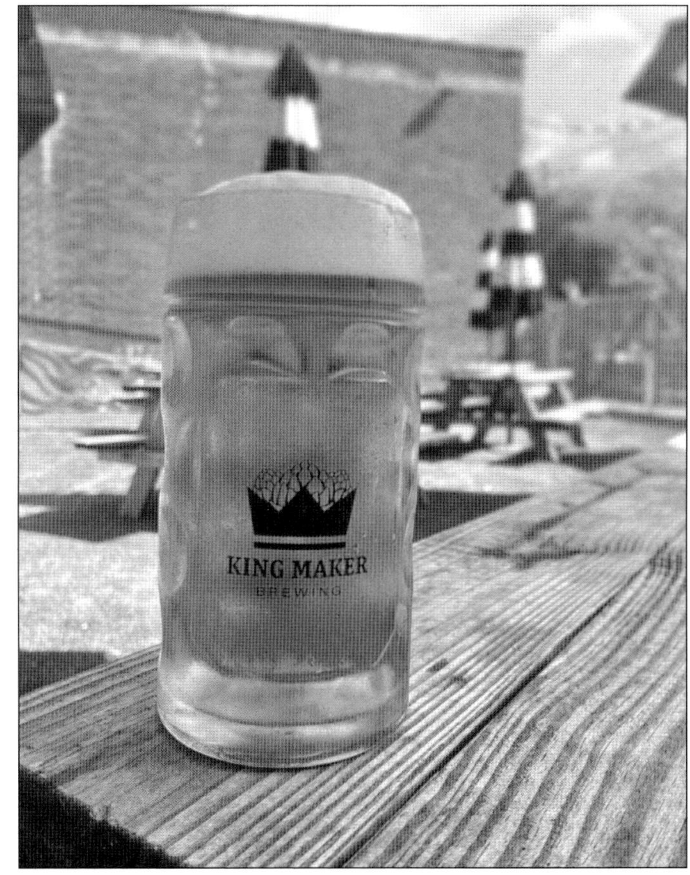

King Maker Brewing was founded in 2020 by James Menker on King Street. The tap room that King Maker is in dates to 1928, and its adjacent warehouse dates to the 1950s. Beers brewed by King Maker include 1913 Czech dark lager, Dortmuner export lager, Riverside Kid Helles bock, 100 Cursing Parrots IPA, Royal Red Irish red ale, and Tangerine Sour. (Courtesy of Andrew R. Nicholas.)

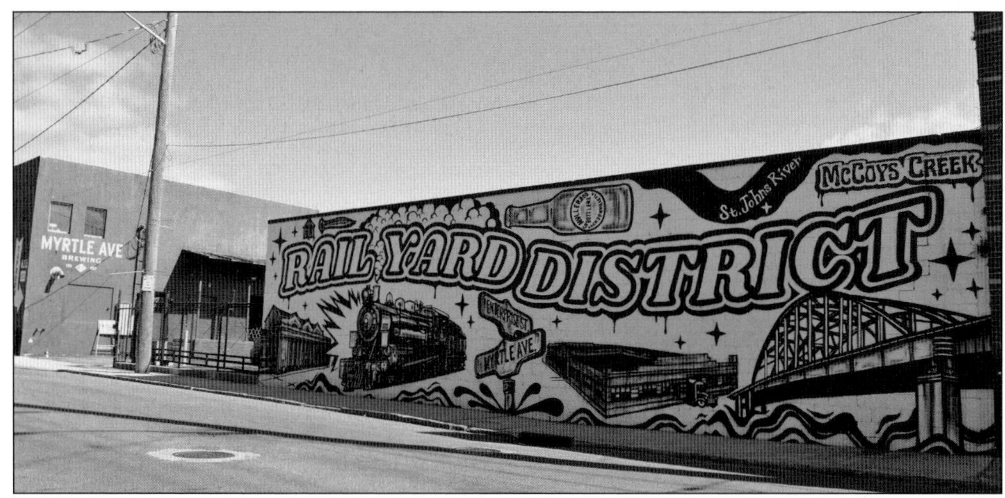

Myrtle Avenue Brewing Company was opened in 2022 by Sean Bielman, the cofounder of Engine 15 Brewing Company, and James Menker in the Rail Yard District of Jacksonville. The brewery was established at Engine 15 Brewing Company's former second location on Myrtle Avenue. Beers brewed by Myrtle Avenue Brewing include Silver Lining's IPA, Samuel Jacksonville Lager, LaVilla Sour, Emerald Trail IPA, and Gutenbier lager. (Courtesy of Andrew R. Nicholas.)

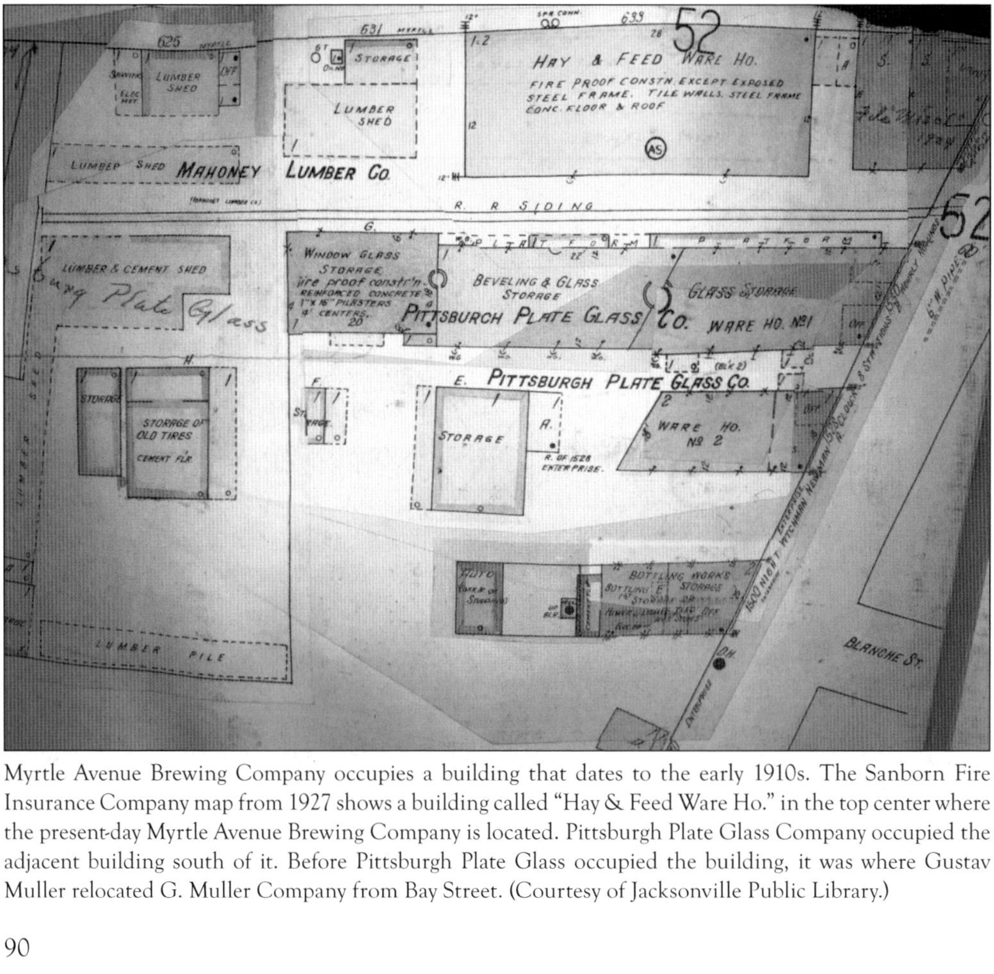

Myrtle Avenue Brewing Company occupies a building that dates to the early 1910s. The Sanborn Fire Insurance Company map from 1927 shows a building called "Hay & Feed Ware Ho." in the top center where the present-day Myrtle Avenue Brewing Company is located. Pittsburgh Plate Glass Company occupied the adjacent building south of it. Before Pittsburgh Plate Glass occupied the building, it was where Gustav Muller relocated G. Muller Company from Bay Street. (Courtesy of Jacksonville Public Library.)

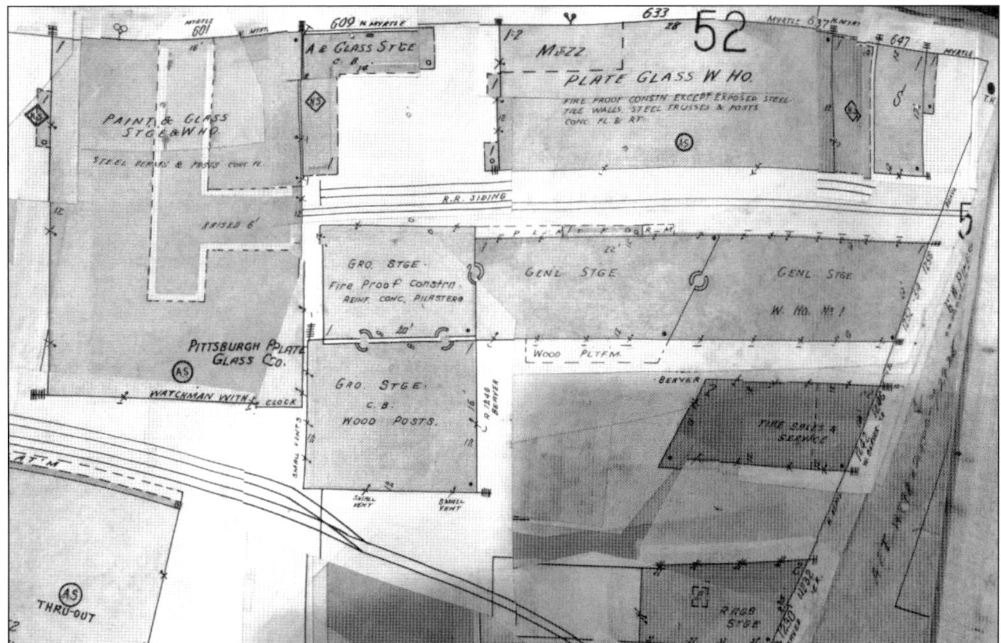

Adjacent to Myrtle Avenue Brewing Company is a wedding and event venue called the Glass Factory. The Glass Factory building was built in 1936 and designed by renowned Jacksonville architect Henry Klutho. This Sanborn Insurance map from 1942 shows Pittsburgh Plate Glass occupying Klutho's building with its warehouse called the "Plate Glass W. Ho" on the map where present-day Myrtle Avenue Brewing Company is located. (Courtesy of Jacksonville Public Library.)

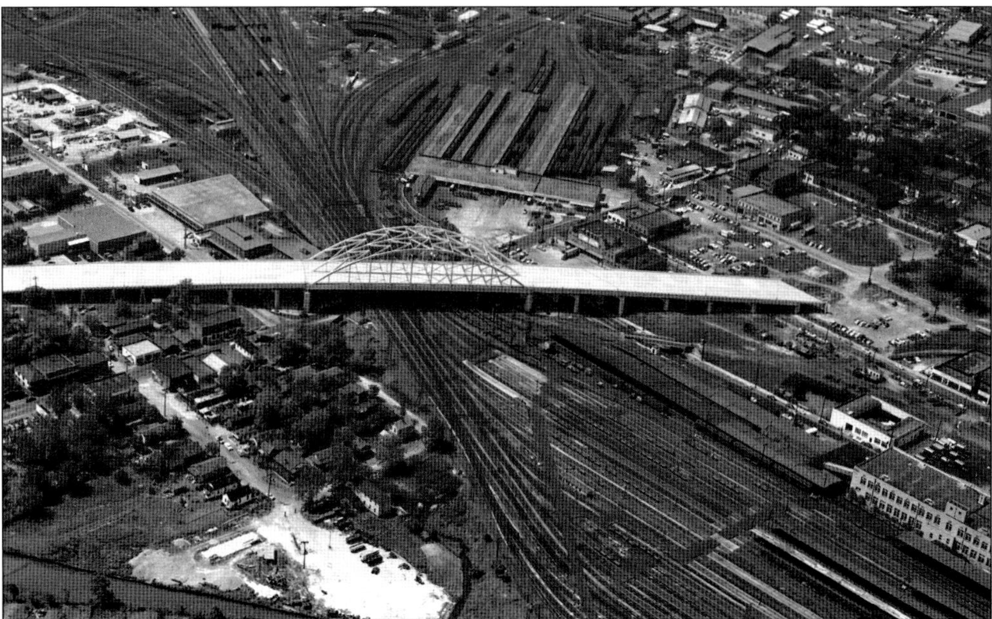

The logo of Myrtle Avenue Brewing Company features the nearby Myrtle Avenue Overpass. The steel arch overpass was built in 1955 and carries Interstate 95 over Myrtle Avenue and railroads. The photograph of the Myrtle Avenue Overpass was taken in 1958. The present-day building of Myrtle Avenue Brewing can be seen near the upper-right corner. (Courtesy of State Archives of Florida.)

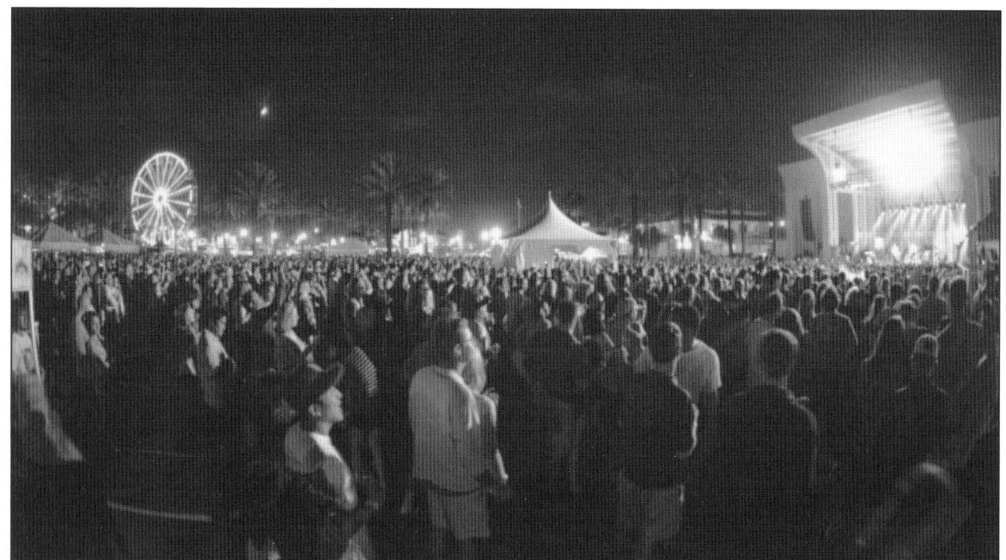

Oktoberfest began in 1810 as a wedding celebration between Bavaria's Crown Prince Ludwig and Princess Therese of Saxony-Hildburghausen. That celebration later turned into an annual event notable for becoming a beer festival held in Munich, Bavaria, Germany. Worldwide, there are many Oktoberfest celebrations, including the Beaches Oktoberfest festival in Jacksonville Beach. The photograph shows a live band performing during the Beaches Oktoberfest at the Seawalk Pavilion in Jacksonville Beach in 2023. (Courtesy of Beaches Oktoberfest.)

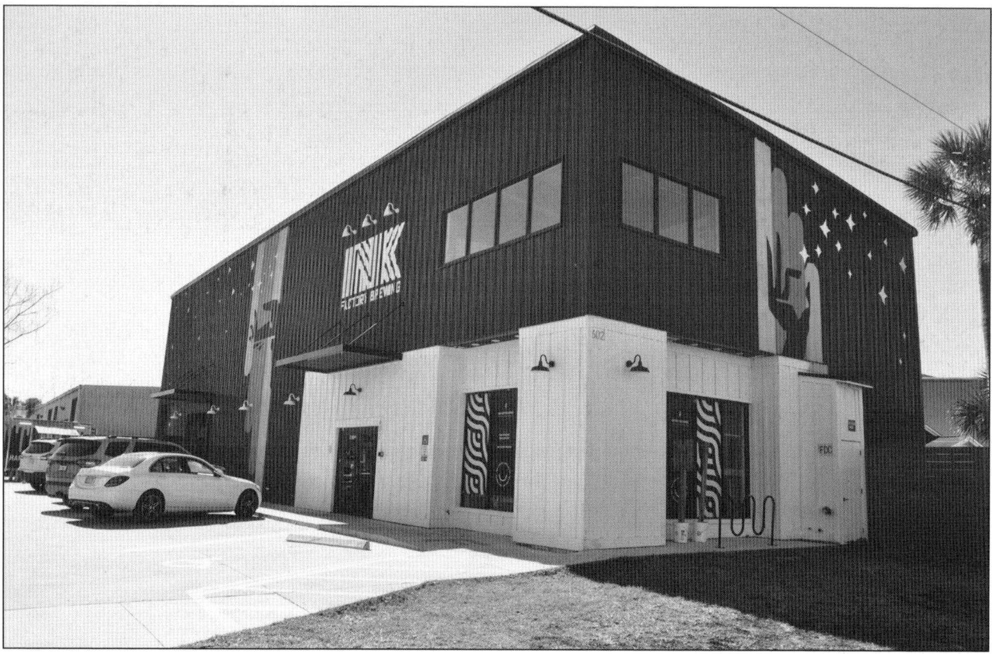

Ink Factory Brewing was opened in 2022 by Aaron Meisenheimer and Ty Wallace in Jacksonville Beach. Meisenheimer and Wallace had previously started a local magazine for the Jacksonville area called *Void* in 2010, but due to the economic effects of the COVID-19 pandemic, it ended publication in 2021. The former *Void* magazine warehouse was thereafter renovated into Ink Factory Brewing. (Courtesy of Andrew R. Nicholas.)

Grace Note Brewing was opened in 2023 as a music-themed brewery by Jeremy Baker and James Trimble of the Jacksonville pop punk band Inspection 12. It is Jacksonville's first music-themed brewery. The photograph shows Grace Note Brewing beers Perfect Pitch hazy IPA, Cut Time double IPA, The Jam English pale ale, and Boleslaus Grodziskie smoked wheat table beer. The brewery opened in the Lake Shore neighborhood by the Ortega River. (Courtesy of Grace Note Brewing.)

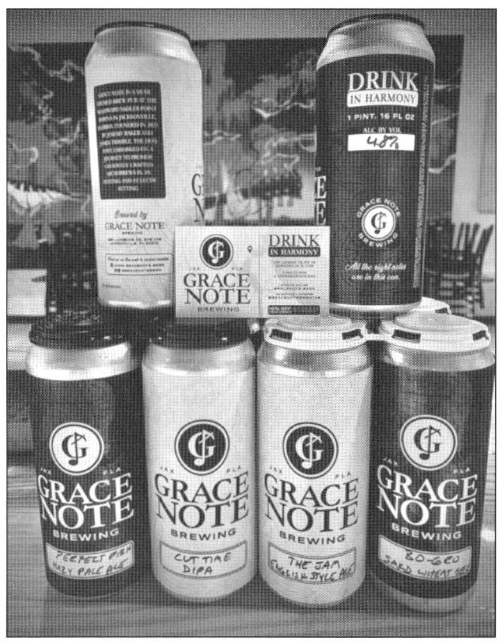

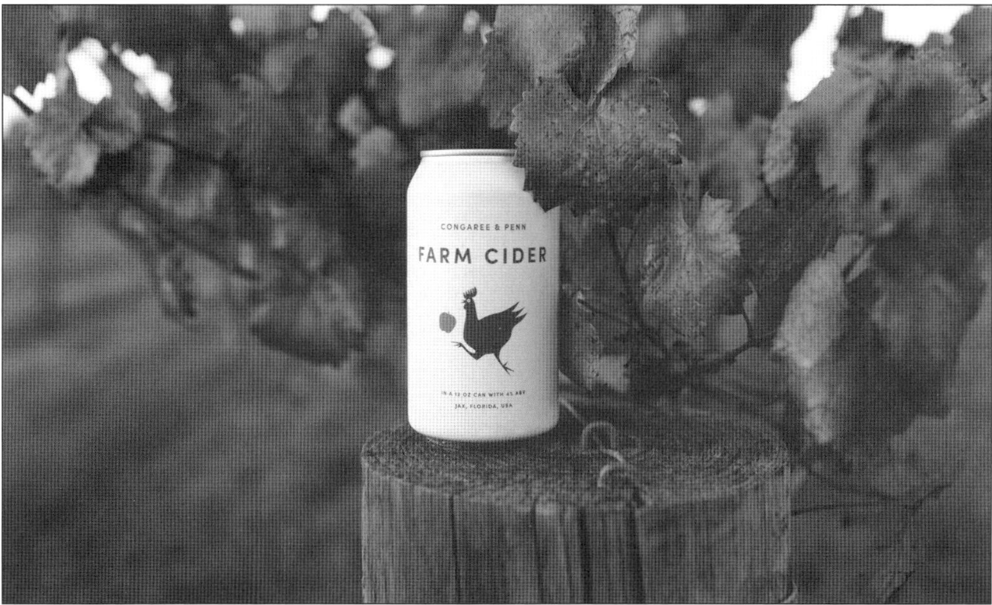

Congaree & Penn first began in 2014 as a rice farm and mill 12 miles outside downtown Jacksonville. It was founded by Scott Meyer after he graduated with a master's in aquaculture, the science of fish farming. His father, Jeff Meyer, had acquired the land and operated it as a tree farm. After the success of Meyer's rice farming, he decided to plant muscadine grape and mayhaw trees to brew and distill beverages like cider. Congaree & Penn's Farm Cider is made from a locally grown orchard. "Congaree" comes from USS *Congaree*, which was captained by Scott Meyer's grandfather. "Penn" comes from Pennington, his mother's maiden name. The farm of Congaree & Penn has grown from its early days as a rice farm into 330 acres with a restaurant, event space, wagon rides, a Quonset hut, agritourism, and a distillery. The photograph shows a Farm Cider can at the Congaree & Penn farm. The cider is distributed throughout Jacksonville stores and bars. (Courtesy of Stefanie Keeler, Congaree & Penn.)

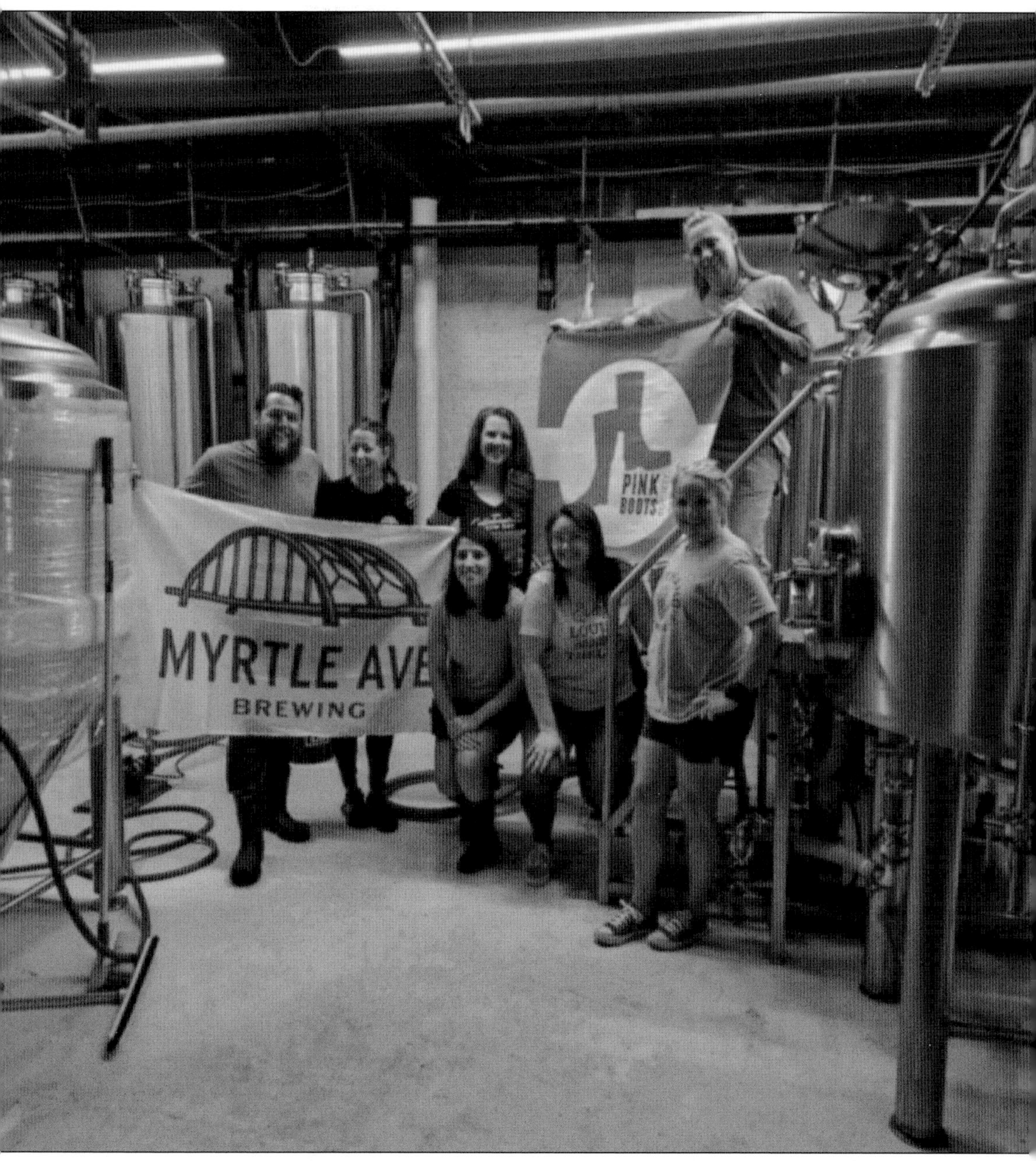

The Pink Boots Society is a nonprofit organization that supports women and nonbinary people to further their education in the brewing industry since 2007. The organization has chapters throughout the United States, Canada, Europe, Peru, Australia, and New Zealand. The photograph shows the local Jacksonville Pink Boots Society at Myrtle Avenue Brewing. (Courtesy of Myrtle Avenue Brewing.)

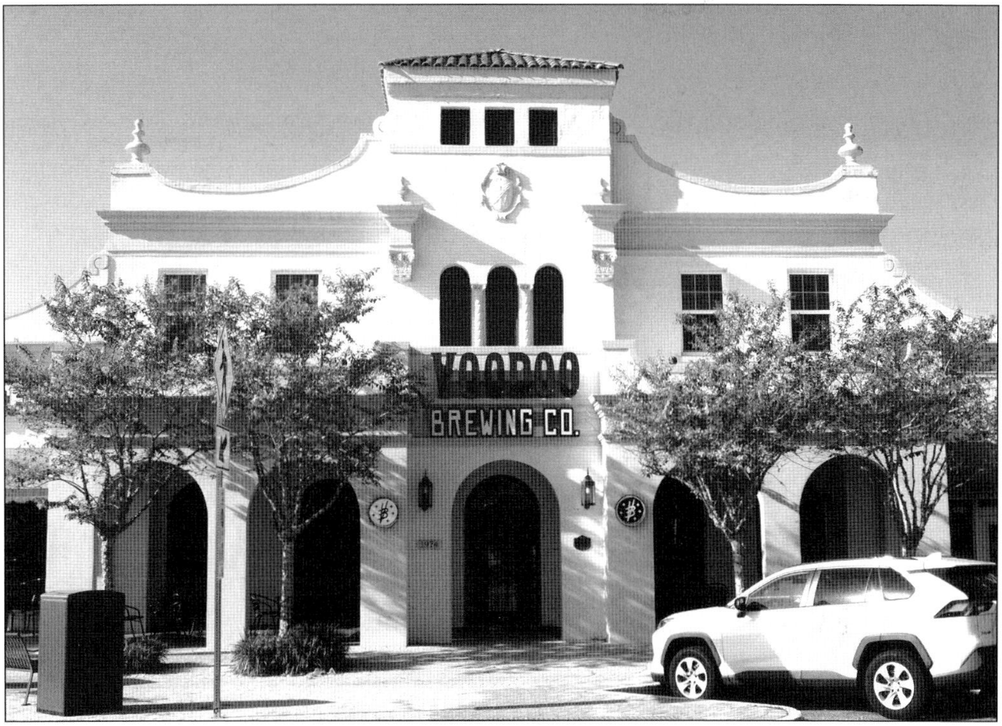

Voodoo Brewing Company was established in 2005 in Meadville, Pennsylvania. The growth of Voodoo Brewing Company years after it first began led to additional expansions outside of Pennsylvania with locations in Ohio, North Carolina, South Carolina, Colorado, and Nevada. In 2024, the first Voodoo Brewing Company location in Florida opened in the San Marco building. Over $800,000 in renovations were done to the building to turn it into a brewery. Beers brewed at Voodoo Brewing include White Magick of the Sun ale, Thunder Lizard IPA, Oh Mama lager, Wynona's Big Brown Ale, and I'm a Loner Dottie, a Rebel IPA. (Courtesy of Andrew R. Nicholas.)

The San Marco building was built in 1926–1927 and was designed by Marsh & Saxelbye. It was the first commercial building on San Marco Square. The building was first referred to as Towne Pump when it housed a business called Towne Pump Drugs and Sundries. In the 1960s, the building became a bar and lounge called the Town Pump. (Courtesy of Jacksonville Historic Preservation Commission.)

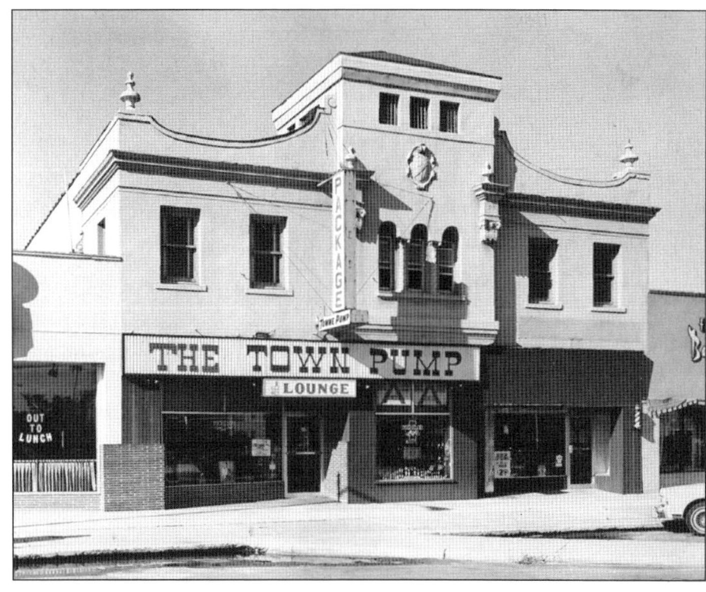

DISCOVER THOUSANDS OF LOCAL HISTORY BOOKS FEATURING MILLIONS OF VINTAGE IMAGES

Arcadia Publishing, the leading local history publisher in the United States, is committed to making history accessible and meaningful through publishing books that celebrate and preserve the heritage of America's people and places.

Find more books like this at
www.arcadiapublishing.com

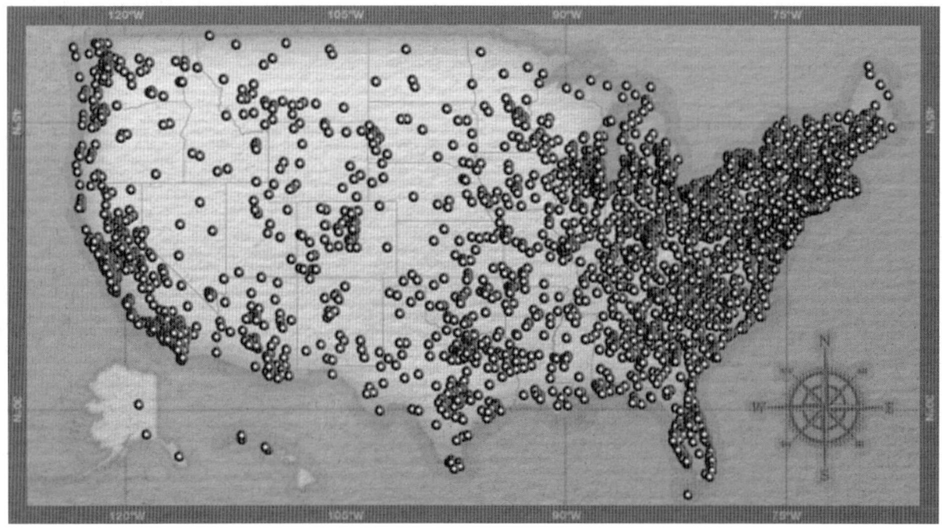

Search for your hometown history, your old stomping grounds, and even your favorite sports team.

Consistent with our mission to preserve history on a local level, this book was printed in South Carolina on American-made paper and manufactured entirely in the United States. Products carrying the accredited Forest Stewardship Council (FSC) label are printed on 100 percent FSC-certified paper.

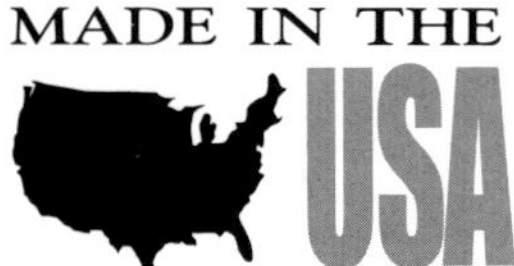